Fishing for BIG CHUB

Fishing for
BIG CHUB
Peter Stone

Beekay Publishers

Also by Beekay Publishers:
Carp Fever by Kevin Maddocks
Success with the Pole by Dickie Carr
Pike Fishing in the 80's by Neville Fickling
Basic Carp Fishing by Peter Mohan
Modern Specimen Hunting by Jim Gibbinson
Top Ten edited by Bruce Vaughan

*(All titled available direct from the publishers.
See inside back cover for details.)*

First published 1983 by
BEEKAY PUBLISHERS
103 Worcesters Avenue
Enfield, EN1 4ND
©Peter Stone 1983

Printed and bound by
Castle Cary Press Ltd., Castle Cary, Somerset

ISBN 0 9507598 6 4

Contents

Introduction		9
Chapter 1	Behaviour	13
Chapter 2	Tackle	21
Chapter 3	Baits	29
Chapter 4	Location	39
Chapter 5	Rivers	41
Chapter 6	Ice holes	79
Chapter 7	Stillwaters	83
Chapter 8	The River Annan	103
Chapter 9	Chub rivers and big chub list	107
Chapter 10	My biggest chub	117

Acknowledgements

My thanks are due to the Editor of Coarse Fishing Monthly for permission to use articles already published; to Jim Gibbinson for permission to quote from his book 'Chub'; to Len Arbery for supplying the Top 50 Chub list; to Gerry Hughes for the picture of the 8½lb chub; to Dick Walker for reading the original manuscript and to Kevin Maddocks for his help and encouragement and final acceptance of this book for publication.

To my friends who in various ways have helped, especially Dennis Moss and Peter Carpenter who left their firesides to photograph my 7¼lb chub and to my regular fishing companion Geoff Barnes — the very best of companions — for all his help and the many happy hours we have spent together.

Lastly, but by no means least, to my wife Sue who encourages me in every possible way.

A 4lb 12oz Windrush fish — the author's only bite that day.

The end of a satisfying morning — a four-pounder.

Introduction

I am often asked whether I have a favourite fish and the answer is no. There are many species and situations which excite me; a big bream wallowing on the surface, a two-pound roach specially when taken from a river, and catching tench in gravel pits, is what I enjoy most. If, however, I was obliged to fish for one species only for the rest of my days, one stands over all others — chub.

Not that chub could be called great fighters, but they eat almost anything, they can be caught on most methods and 'snowbroth' (water coloured by melting snow) excepted, they feed in all weathers — an obliging fish if ever there was one. Chub however — big chub especially — are shy and anglers who catch them consistently, particularly from small waters, need have no fears about their stealth and approach. Obliging fish chub may be, but they are cunning; big still-water chub especially so.

Initially I was undecided as to what form this book should take; from a beginner's point of view, from a specialist's with the emphasis on big chub (4lbs and over) or for the middle of the road angler. I eventually decided to assume the reader had passed the beginners stage, and wished to increase his knowledge and catch more and bigger chub. Although the book leans towards big chub the methods described will catch medium-sized fish too. Not everyone wishes to spend hours in search of one big fish, most anglers are happy just catching chub irrespective of size and I have written the book with this in mind.

In recent years an ever-increasing number of anglers have turned their attention to gravel pits in which chub often grow to an enormous size. From the late 70's onwards very big chub have been taken from pits on deadbaits intended for pike. Many anglers were surprised by this but having caught many chub on fish long before I left school this came as no surprise to me. To the majority of anglers brought up on maggots, and to a lesser extent bread, catching chub on fish baits was something new and I hope the reader having read the chapter on stillwaters will try dead fish because where *outsize* chub are concerned deadbaiting is a very effective method indeed.

Stillwater chub, however, are extremely shy with thought, planning and sometimes special rigs being necessary to outwit them. It is a slow game too but when you finally find yourself gazing down at that great bronze flank all the biteless hours are quickly forgotten.

Although there is a chapter on tackle I have not gone too deeply into it because I don't wish to 'talk down' to the reader. What I will say however is that at *all times* tackle must be perfect, and while the best of tackle will never turn a mediocre angler into a good one, inferior tackle will not only hamper your progress but result in fish being lost. And no-one likes losing fish, especially big ones.

Swingtips and springtips are omitted. Although they have a part —often a big one—to play in legering techniques I have never found them necessary where chub are concerned. Waters no doubt exist where swingtips pay off: a heavily-fished water where, say, legered casters are necessary to catch them with minute bites the order of the day. Here, a swingtip might outscore other methods but I don't know of one and I only write from experience.

In chapter 3 I discuss baits. Although sweetcorn is not mentioned, in stillwaters this is a bait worth persevering with because several big chub have been taken on this bait. I don't know any water where tench refuse sweetcorn and a swim fished with corn, specially if pre-baited, could result in some remarkable catches.

Weather, I made little reference to. As I said earlier, chub feed in all kinds, and although some days weather does affect their feeding I don't consider it terribly important although that is not to say some conditions and times are not more favourable than others. In some pits for instance chub, especially big ones, feed mainly at night where daytime fishing is often a waste of time. In rivers, early mornings and evenings are often best; conversely, when using floating crust the midday hours—no matter how hot it is—are often better.

Jim Gibbinson once said if you fancy your chances go, no matter what the weather, and there is much truth in that. My first ten-pound bream came on a bitterly cold September night when I sat facing an east wind, but I had that 'feeling'. My biggest chub also came in an east wind—and with a bright moon too—far from ideal conditions. But on both occasions I wanted to go so although weather does have a role to play it should never influence you.

In the 1960's Peter Drennan—then a very youthful Drennan—and I journeyed to Christchurch in Hampshire to spend a week fishing with the late Bill Warren. Among the array of stuffed fish in Bill's hallway was a 7lb 6oz chub which Bill caught on the Royalty in 1957. I spent much time that week gazing—I admit in awe—at that great chub and during the years following wondered whether one day a 'seven' would come my way.

One day in January '82 on the banks of a pit I met Philip Tew from London who a few days earlier had caught a seven pounder. "I'm writing a book about chub", I told Philip, "and would like a seven—just to wrap the whole thing up". Not that I *had* to catch a seven-pound chub to write a book about them. A carp angler doesn't have to catch a 'forty' or a roach angler a 'three' to write on their respective favourites. Providing they have caught plenty of good-sized fish with a few 'biggies' among them, that I think is sufficient recommendation to put pen to paper. And that, with all modesty, is what I have achieved; countless numbers of four pounders, a few 'fives', three 'sixes' and one 'seven'. I started this book some two years ago then when almost complete, I thought a 'seven' would put the icing on the cake. My search for that elusive 'seven' began in November '81; four months later one picked up my bait and shortly after the book was 'wrapped up'.

One drawback when writing specialist books is that by the time they are published the author has added to his knowledge and this book is no exception. I am penning this on a cold, wet, windy day in March when I should have been fishing. But fishing is meant to be enjoyed and I *don't* enjoy fishing in wind *and* rain together. Pete Drennan has called round and our chat got around to dead-baiting for chub in pits, the outcome being that Pete is making some floats which will enable me to fish deadbaits off the bottom at distance. That, and a special bait mix are just two ideas floating around in my head and if this book reaches a second edition I shall have more to tell.

Non-angling friends have often remarked upon the amount of patience anglers have: "How you can sit there all that time doing nothing I cannot understand", has been said to me more times than I can remember. But I am not a patient man and while some anglers are content "just sitting there doing nothing", that is not so in my case. Long biteless hours I abhor; sitting over a static deadbait is the most boring fishing I know, but I am not "just sitting there doing nothing"—I'm thinking, thinking what I can do, if not at that moment, to hasten a bite. 'Patience is an angler's virtue' it is said; maybe, but Dick Walker summed it up perfectly when he said it is not patience that is needed but *controlled impatience*. I could not put it better.

All this is fun. I put much effort and time into my fishing but I enjoy it and if the day ever comes when fishing ceases to be enjoyment I shall stop: never should fishing be a chore; at all times it must be fun, and exciting too. Several years ago Dick Walker landed a double-figure trout at Avington (one of many big trout Dick had taken from that water) and as Dick unhooked it Alan Pearson who was watching said, "Do you know, my cock—you're shaking". To which Dick replied, "When the day comes when a big fish does not cause me to shake I'll pack up". And Dick has caught his share of big fish.

In 1968 the Record Fish Committee acclaimed Bill Warren's chub as the British record. Bill's record is, however, vulnerable and I don't think it will be long before a bigger—probably a lot bigger—chub is caught and properly witnessed. While a few rivers like the Wye, the Annan and possibly the Kennet are capable of producing a new record there is, I think, little doubt that a new record will come from a gravel pit, and I'll be honest: such a fish figures very much in my plans!

Forty-odd years of fishing, many of them spent in pursuit of chub, has given me much fun, excitement, big fish—and many shaking hands. God willing, there are many more to come.

1. Behaviour

Many consider chub the shyest of all our fish but that is debatable. While in some waters—stillwaters in particular—their shyness is almost beyond belief, in others it is less so. Although I have fished for carp I am not a carp fisherman but I believe that, generally speaking, the shyness of carp is greater than that of chub. But like chub, carp—often big ones who should know better—can be very easy indeed. Fred Towns once nobbled an eighteen-pounder which took a piece of crust in very shallow water under his rod tip while tench fishing, in a water where they were extremely difficult to catch. In August 1982 another friend, Pete Carpenter, took a twenty-seven pounder (which he could see) within thirty seconds of casting; I could go on. But like carp, chub at most times display extreme shyness and the angler should at all times approach his quarry with that firmly in his mind.

The normal behaviour of chub is to disappear or stop feeding immediately they suspect all is not well. Being by nature a shoal fish, immediately one becomes suspicious the others become agitated—a clear case of 'follow the leader'. Because of that the capture of, say, 50lb of chub at a sitting is considered something of an angling feat. While you may take, say, up to a dozen from a swim, by the time the last fish has made its mistake the others, realising something is amiss, 'disappear'. To counteract this, matchmen, after catching two or three, often 'rest' the swim for a while, fishing another 'line' so as not to disturb the others—an excellent ploy which specimen hunters could well adopt.

Close to my home is a weirpool where fishing is strictly prohibited. The pool is full of chub between two and four pounds which are hand-fed every day. They are 'tame', taking anything given them—even cigarette ends! On odd occasions to assist my research of chub behaviour the owners have kindly allowed me to fish the pool. The

A chub attempting to take a piece of bread off ranunculus—almost on 'dry land'.

first time I fished under the rod top; caught four in as many casts, then nothing. Determined not to make the same mistake again, the next time I fished from the opposite bank some 25 yards away, which would allow me to pull them away quickly from the others and therefore not disturb them. That's what I *thought*, mind: that morning I caught five in five casts but no more. Walking round to where I had been casting I peered over the wall: where less than half an hour before there had been dozens now there were none. Later that day, hours after I had departed, I returned for a look-see. Having got over their early morning fright they were back taking without hesitation the pieces of bread I gave them while standing less than ten feet away.

The most amazing demonstration of behaviour I ever witnessed occurred one summer evening in a Thames backwater. A friend, Bob Hastings, rang imploring me to go and look at some chub which he said were "taking bread on dry land". Exactly what Bob meant I wasn't sure but an hour later I was at the scene with tackle, a loaf of bread and my cameras. The river at this point was some 30ft wide, the surface almost covered by ranunculus (streamer weed). Under the weed a shoal of chub were in residence, a few of which periodically moved out into a small patch of open water before returning to cover again.

It was not however the chub which ventured out from under the weed which were interesting but those under it, and during the following hour I witnessed something the like of which I doubt I shall ever see again. At Bob's suggestion I threw several pieces of crust, matchbox-size, on top of the dense weed. Minutes later 'humps' appeared under the weed by one of the pieces of bread followed by the lips of a chub (sometimes several) appearing through the dense weed. The lips were followed by the eyes, then the gills, then the head; then, with the chub's head completely exposed the fish lunged forward, grabbed the crust and disappeared back under the weed. Sometimes a chub having started too far back and finding itself several inches behind the crust would expose its shoulder and on one occasion — which I was too late to photograph — part of its body too in order to reach the crust. After shooting an entire film we started fishing and finished with a big bag on floating crust presented just outside the weedbed, but fishing that evening took second place. It was, and still is, the most remarkable and fascinating display of chub behaviour I have ever seen.

In the past, many writers have said that once the frosts set in chub remain close to the bottom, remaining there for most of the winter. Because a bait presented on, or close to, the bottom in winter is on many days the tactic to employ, to say — as many writers still do — that chub will not take food on, or close to, the surface in winter, is nonsense.

One day I was fishing the Thames; it was in flood and immediately below me and against my bank was a raft of rubbish, against which for some reason which escapes me I threw several pieces of crust. Shortly after a s...u...c...k came from the raft and looking round I was just in time to see one crust disappear. That a chub should rise to the surface in high, coloured, water for a piece of crust was, in view of what I had read (and believed) over the years, surprising, but when several weeks later again in coloured water I caught a chub on floating crust in similar circumstances I realized it was no fluke. Shortly after, Jack Hilton penned an article in which he described catching chub amongst grass and herbage in flood water which left me in no doubt that chub took food off the surface in winter more than I realised. Since then I have caught chub on floating crust with snow

After hooking this near five-pound chub (on floating crust) the author gave his rod to the angler (left) who landed it.

thick on the ground (in clear water); on casters and maggots under a float, fished 3ft deep over 14ft of water and on one occasion on floating crust in a narrow channel between thick ice over 12ft of water.

Earlier I remarked on the chub's shyness. But as in most things there are exceptions and an experience of mine with a huge chub in a gravel pit in the summer of 1981 is worth relating. Like chub in many gravel pits, the shyness of those in this particular pit is almost beyond belief and most days you cannot get within fifty yards of them. On this particular day I had spent the morning tench fishing; mid-afternoon came, it was hot and my foodbox had long been empty. Time for home I reckoned, and five minutes later I was walking back to my car. A few days previously in the same pit I had seen a very big chub lying on a 'bar'. I was now approaching that bar and thinking a chub might be on the bar sunning itself I slackened my pace. As I reached the bar—which was concealed by a high bank—I slacked my pace even more and by the time I had reached the high bank I was almost at a standstill. The first thing I saw was the rear end of a swan pointing skywards as it groped on the bottom right in the spot where I expected a chub might be. It was too much and I admit, in a moment of anger, I picked up a stone and threw it. Startled, the swan turned four complete circles flapping its wings furiously then set off up the pit. But that was not all: in the *exact* spot where the swan had been was a huge chub!

I could not believe it; after such a commotion no self-respecting chub should be in the vicinity let alone the actual spot. But a chub *was* there—and not just a four-pounder either! For several seconds I just 'froze', waiting for it to swim off. But it didn't, and slowly the thought came to me I might just nobble it. Retreating slowly—oh, so slowly—backwards I got well back in the grass and I admit with shaking fingers tackled up again: 3lb b.s. line, a two swan-shot Pete Drennan 'Loader' float, number 8 hook and flake. Creeping back I peered over; the chub was still there. It looked about six feet down so the question was how far away should I cast; far enough not to frighten it but close enough for the flake to be intercepted before it reached the end of its drop. Fourteen feet, ten, eight?—I settled for ten, which as it turned out was two feet too many.

On hearing the 'plop' the chub turned and swam slowly towards the slowly sinking flake. The chub didn't hurry itself—another point in its favour—but I was already thinking it was mine. With the chub some two feet away the flake reached the limit of its drop and a second later when the chub reached it, it was suspended. With its fins quivering ('on the fin' as trout fishermen say) the chub looked closely at the flake, circled it twice then, to my great sorrow, departed.

That experience (and others) demonstrates quite clearly the importance of presentation and, when you can see your quarry, of judging distance accurately. Fishing flake 'on the drop' is a deadly method of taking big chub in stillwaters, easily outscoring floating crust especially on calm days when chub are frightened of the line on the surface no matter how thin it is. But with the line sunk, flake does not throw up such problems but the cast has to be *dead* right (see chapter 7). That day just *two* feet cost me the chub of a lifetime.

In chapter 7 I describe the methods on which I and others have caught big chub on dead fish. Yet despite the chub's liking for fish—dead or alive—the number of anglers who use fish baits is still comparatively low. Chub are great fish eaters and many of my biggest river specimens have fallen to freelined bleak and gudgeon during the summer. Many of these have been taken from the Thames and Cherwell which I find rather strange because in these rivers—and there are no doubt others—weirpools excepted, to fish bread or cheese on the bottom is most days a waste of time. But if chub will take fish off the bottom why not bread and cheesepaste?

Stillwater chub as I said earlier are extremely shy, yet days occur when like big bream they lose much of their caution, showing almost suicidal tendencies. During the autumn of 1979 a friend, Dennis Moss, noticed a shoal of big chub on a bar harassing fry—the period when big chub lose some of their caution. Fishing floating crust (a good bait when chub are 'frying') in under two hours Dennis put eight chub between four and five and a quarter pounds on the bank. Now that was a remarkable catch, but in a water where, on average, you are lucky to catch two in a *season* it was bloody remarkable!

In chapter 7 I mention chub which I have seen cruising and lying against my rod rest in stillwaters at night and in chapter 10 where by fishing a bait close in I caught a near-record fish. Over the years I have fished several pits which hold outsize chub and in one they are particularly difficult. On the rare occasions you see one in daytime it is always a long way out—most times well out of casting range—typical big-chub behaviour in stillwaters. Walk around the pit at dawn however and somewhere, often in several places, at least one big chub can be seen lying in the margins, and one morning Geoff Barnes put one on the bank (see chapter 7). Immediately I had established these bankside sorties were commonplace behaviour I set about catching one, and although it took over a year my dream of catching a huge chub just past the rod top was eventually realised (see chapter 10). That, however, is only a start; other ideas are already floating around in my head, ideas which will I hope in the future result in more outsize chub sliding towards my waiting net.

When snow is around is often a good time to be abroad

2. Tackle

In 1956 I designed a rod for legering because at that time there was not a rod available commercially that fulfilled my needs: i.e. light enough to hold all day without fatigue, and one which — important this — had a very fine tip but which was capable of landing big fish.

My rod, called the 'Legerstrike', was made from built cane, two joints, and 10ft in length. Following some spectacular catches, rod manufacturer Ron Chapman asked to see it, liked what he saw, and asked if he could produce it commercially. The rod became Ron's best seller and he later made a glass version. In the early 60's Davenport and Fordham made the rod then, when they eventually closed, Modern Arms. The 'Legerstrike' became the 'Ultra-lite' — by then I had added another 15 inches to it — and in 1981 Tony Fordham and I decided to handle the rod ourselves. Today, twenty-three years on, the 11¼ft 'Ultra-lite' continues to sell — and catch big fish.

I tell this because the rod, trotting excepted, is what I use for most of my chubbing and it has accounted for countless numbers of four-pounders, several 'fives' and one 'six'. Having said that, there are of course an abundance of good chubbing rods available but the 'Ultra-lite', the descendant of the 'Legerstrike', has a very soft spot in my heart. For trotting I now use a 12ft Normark carbon model, the extra length being necessary for distance casting and float control.

My reels are Mitchell 410's, lines either Platil, Sylcast Bronze or ABU Matchline. All my floats are made by Pete Drennan. Peter not only makes superb floats, he is a fine angler too and his models fulfill my requirements exactly.

Now hooks; for over twenty years I used Mustad 'Goldstrikes', a superb hook although it is necessary to sharpen them prior to each

Floating crust proved the downfall of this 4¾lb fish.

session. In 1982 Peter Drennan introduced a range of hooks including bronze crystals which in the first week they were used accounted for a 7¼lb chub and several double-figure pike. At the time of writing I have used Peter's hooks for just two months and they are very good, needle sharp, and where chub are concerned I need look no further than Peter's range and Goldstrikes. Alan Bramley, the boss of Partridge, also makes very fine hooks which I dress my flies on and which many specimen hunters use for chub too.

One item of tackle to which insufficient attention is paid is leger stops. Many anglers use split shots but these slip on the strike. In the days when I used shots (but not for long) I often struck at a bite which I was confident of hooking, only to miss. Inspection revealed the shot had slipped and despite what some anglers say, if the stop (whatever it is) slips on the strike, the fish is missed. For years I experimented with different stops and now use the plastic model available in tackle shops. Designed by John Roberts of Kent, this excellent stop consists of a plastic tube ¼in in length and a plastic tapered pin which traps the line in the tube. Initially I thought the pin might pinch the line and cause weakness at that point but it doesn't. When an alteration in the length of tail is desired, the pin should be pushed back out: never attempt to slide the stopper up the line.

For legering in stillwaters I use cork bobbins, some with a Betalite inside for night fishing. My bobbins measure one inch (the length is not important) with a ladies' hair grip through the middle. A length of Dacron line is attached to the bottom of the hair grip, the other end attached to a skewer. The Betalite is attached to one side of the bobbin so it faces towards me when sitting on the left-hand side of the rod.

The only other bite indicator I use is one called the 'Amron' designed and marketed by Robin Evans of Kent. Robin conceived the idea after reading articles (including one of mine) regarding problems with wind blowing the bobbin about. Robin's indicator consists of a clear plastic tube 10ins in length with a spike (removable) to stick it into the ground. The bobbin (which is fluorescent) is attached to a length of nylon with a grip on one end and into which the line is clipped with the bobbin inside the tube. The bobbin is completely unaffected by wind, in which conditions I find it very useful, and I was using one when I caught the 7¼lb chub mentioned in chapter 10.

Although I use quivertips mainly when roach fishing, situations often arise when I use them for chub fishing too, like on very cold

AMRON BITE INDICATOR

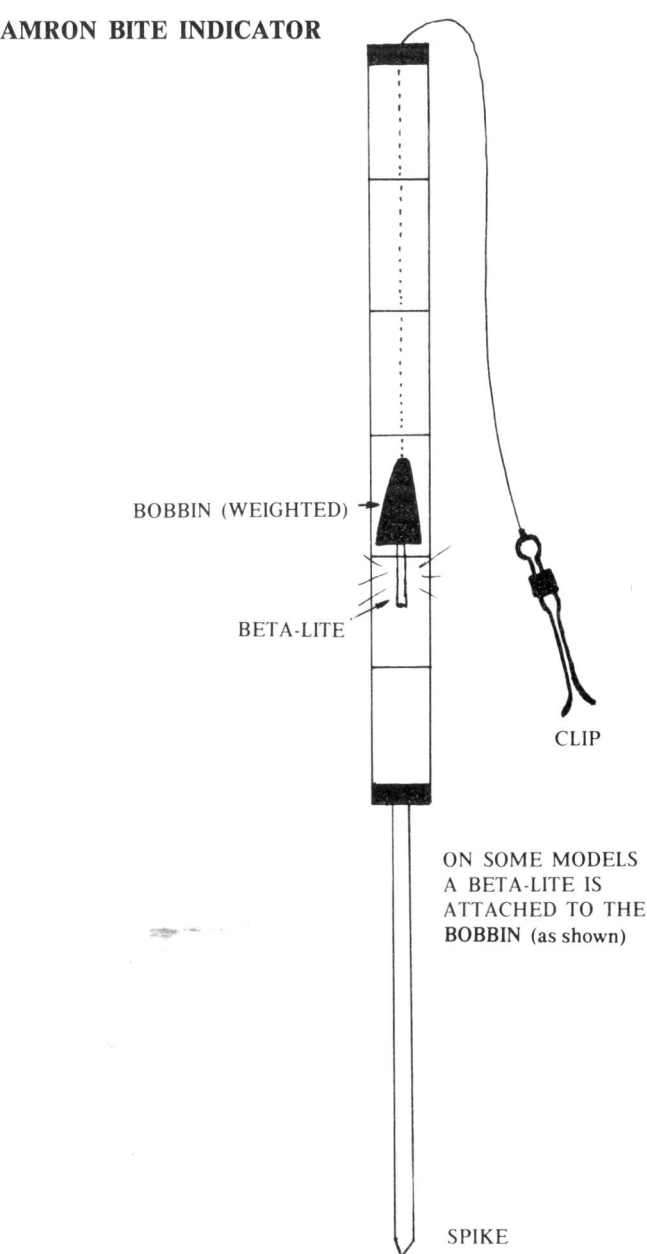

FIG 1

days when bites are likely to be minute. The models I use are Pete Drennan's although in some situations I believe a tapered quiver is better (Peter's are not tapered).

Regarding leads, I use two types: split shot and Arlesey Bombs. Where legering is concerned, for 99 per cent of the time I use shots on a sliding link which I first publicised in 1956. And hereby hangs a tale.... When I first started to leger seriously around 1945 I used a drilled bullet, a lead which despite being popular was, I quickly learnt, a bad lead. At that time I was keen on match fishing and in my club was a leger fishman who I could seldom beat. I hated that: worse still he would never tell me anything—which I hated even more! He caught a lot of chub—big chub—and naturally I was interested in his methods.

As I have said, he would never tell me anything and if I stood behind him (which I often did) he would not remove his tackle from the water. For a teenager as I then was, that was *most* frustrating! Around 1950 he died and a few months later his wife gave me his tackle box. In it were several traces on a winder. On these just above the hook was a split shot and resting against that a short length of nylon with a lead on one end: on the other end, the one nearest the line, was a bead through which the line passed. For the very first time I was looking at a sliding link.

Immediately I made up some links replacing the bead with a split ring. The stopper posed a problem; shots I had already discovered slipped, and after some experimenting I settled for another split ring, which although it entailed two knots at least didn't slip. The advantages of the sliding link were immediately apparent. By using different sizes of split shot it was possible to obtain *exactly* the right amount of weight required: no longer was I restricted to weights the sizes of which varied within ¼oz, for occasions arise when the addition of a BB shot will mean the difference between a blank day and a good one. With the sliding link I could add or remove shots as required. Also, when fishing a stationary bait it did not matter if the lead was buried in rubbish; a fish pulling on the line was pulling only against the rod top *not* the lead as well. The reduced resistance I quickly discovered resulted in more confident, easier-to-hook bites.

During the early 50's my catches using the sliding link improved enormously; better presentation and less vicious bites contributed greatly to my successes both in the field of match fishing and in specimen hunting, in which I was now taking an ever-increasing interest. The news spread, and in 1959 Peter Tombleson and Sonny Cragg, then with *Angling Times*, published a feature of me catching chub on the sliding link—probably the first time ever the sliding link was mentioned in public.

Later, when I began fishing with Dick Walker and the Taylor brothers, Fred adapted the link even further by dispensing with the split ring, simply looping the nylon over the main line with one swan shot against the loop to hold it together. Today the sliding link is used by anglers everywhere and is without doubt one of the major advances ever made in legering techniques.

SLIDING LINK

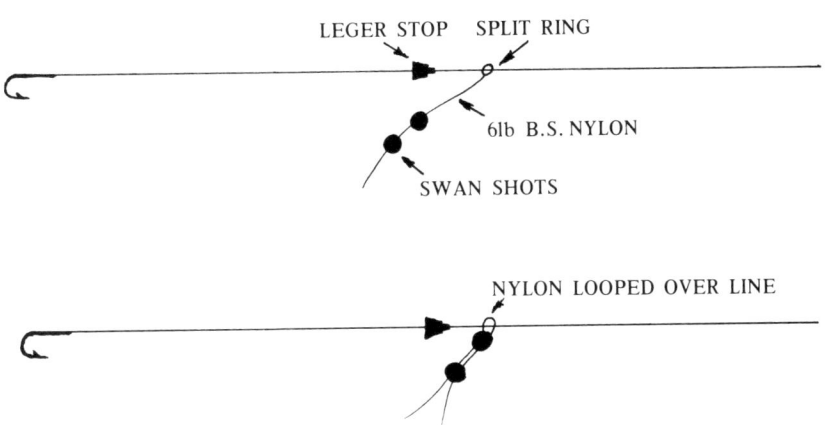

FIG 2

Among several items I would not be without are Beta-lites. I first used one some ten years ago which I attached to the rod top for legering at night; I later incorporated them into my bobbins and later still into some of my floats.

For floats I use a 500 micro-lambert model which can be easily seen up to 30 yards, and for bobbins and rod tops one of 300 micro-lamberts. The first floats I used with Beta-lites inside were for still-water fishing and soon after I considered the possibility of putting them into some of my river floats also. The idea of trotting in the dark appealed, something I had never done mainly because suitable floats were not available. The 'illuminated floats' I had used were, frankly, useless, but a float fitted with a Beta-lite is a different matter entirely.

My first Beta-lite floats were made by Geoff Barnes which I still use, also some of Pete Drennan's commercially-made models. Watching a lighted float in stillwaters is exciting fishing, watching one travelling down a river is *very* exciting! Although as I said earlier, I have 500 micro-lambert Beta-lites in my floats which can be seen at 30 yards, I should make it clear it is rarely necessary to fish at such distances at night — most times ten yards is ample, but a 500 micro-lambert model means much less eye strain with bites easier to see.

Tactics when fishing at night are really little different from those in daylight. Nevertheless there are some rules which should be followed and I will start with the line. Floats fitted with a Beta-lite are expensive, the bulk of the price taken up by the Beta-lite, so you don't want to lose a float if you can help it. To avoid this, use a stronger line than you would in daylight and make sure the line below the float is slightly weaker than the main line. By using a weaker line under the float, should you get snagged or strike too hard, the line will break below the float and not above resulting in its loss. Avoid too, swims which entail casting close to trees, bushes, etc. Accurate casting is much more difficult at night and while chub are seldom found far from cover, fish swims which produce them in daylight.

Now shotting: at night, bites are generally much bolder so shot the float so that all the Beta-lite (about an inch) is above the surface. Should the fish, after taking the bait, rise towards the surface the reflection of the Beta-lite will increase; if the float is pulled under, well . . . one minute the green glow is there, the next it isn't! Should you start fishing before it gets dark (which I advise) difficulty will be experienced seeing the Beta-lite in the period immediately before. During this time a piece of black silicone tubing slipped over the Beta-lite will enable the float to be seen, the rubber being removed once it becomes too dark to see.

Drennan Feederlinks are so well known, description is hardly necessary, but here's a tip. By substituting the ring for a swivel then sliding a length of silicone tubing along the nylon between the swivel and the cap the possibility of tangling is considerably lessened (see Fig 3).

MODIFIED FEEDERLINK

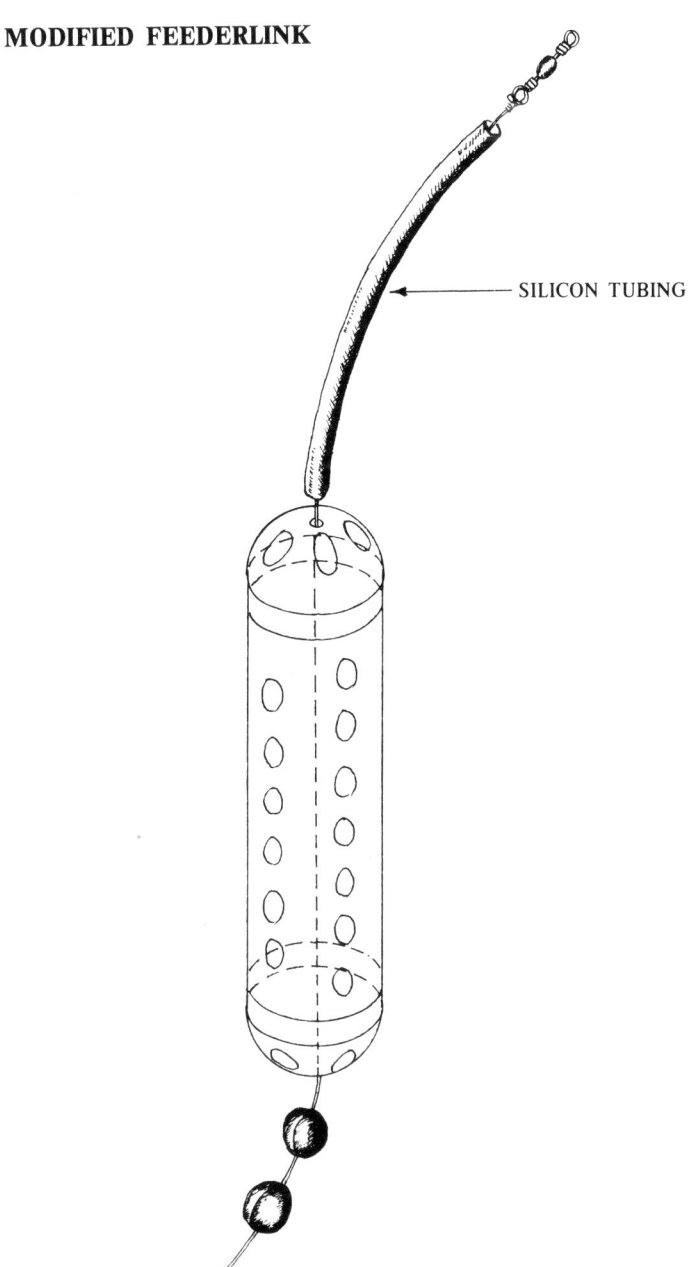

FIG 3

Fishing in tight corners often means bullying tactics too!

3. Baits

To list every bait chub will take is an impossible task and it would take up much less space to list what chub *won't* eat, for their tastes are catholic; very little fails to arouse their interest and I believe that on the occasions when a bait is refused it is, most times, not because of the offering but other factors—like presentation.

So just where *do* you begin when discussing baits? It is, as I have said, difficult, so artificial baits excepted I have decided to confine my list to the most popular ones. These are bread, lobworms, cheese, cheesepaste, sausage and luncheon meat, maggots, casters, hemp (mainly as loose feed), slugs, crayfish, fish, high protein carp baits, and trout pellet paste. Artificial lures are discussed later.

Sausage meat should be mixed with breadcrumbs to a consistency which is soft but not so soft it will not withstand casting. Although chub *will* eat baits which are hard, where sausage meat is concerned, in my experience, chub will reject it if it does not melt in their mouths, so to speak. It is also vital, I find, to ensure there are no lumps of gristle in the bait—not that chub take that much notice but should the gristle attach itself to the hook point penetration can be affected. The size of the bait (not just with sausage meat but other 'paste' baits too) depends upon the hook size, for at all times the hook must fit the bait—i.e. a walnut-sized piece on a number 4.

Luncheon meat should be cut into squares, the size depending on what you consider the chub will accept at a given time. Most times I round off the edges which might make a difference—on the other hand it may not! If the meat has no 'sharp' edges I feel better and if I feel right, I fish better.

Lobworms should be fished with the hook passed through the head *once*, not two or three times thus tying the worm in a knot. Like worms, slugs are hooked once. How to hook crayfish is discussed in chapter 5 and fish in chapter 7.

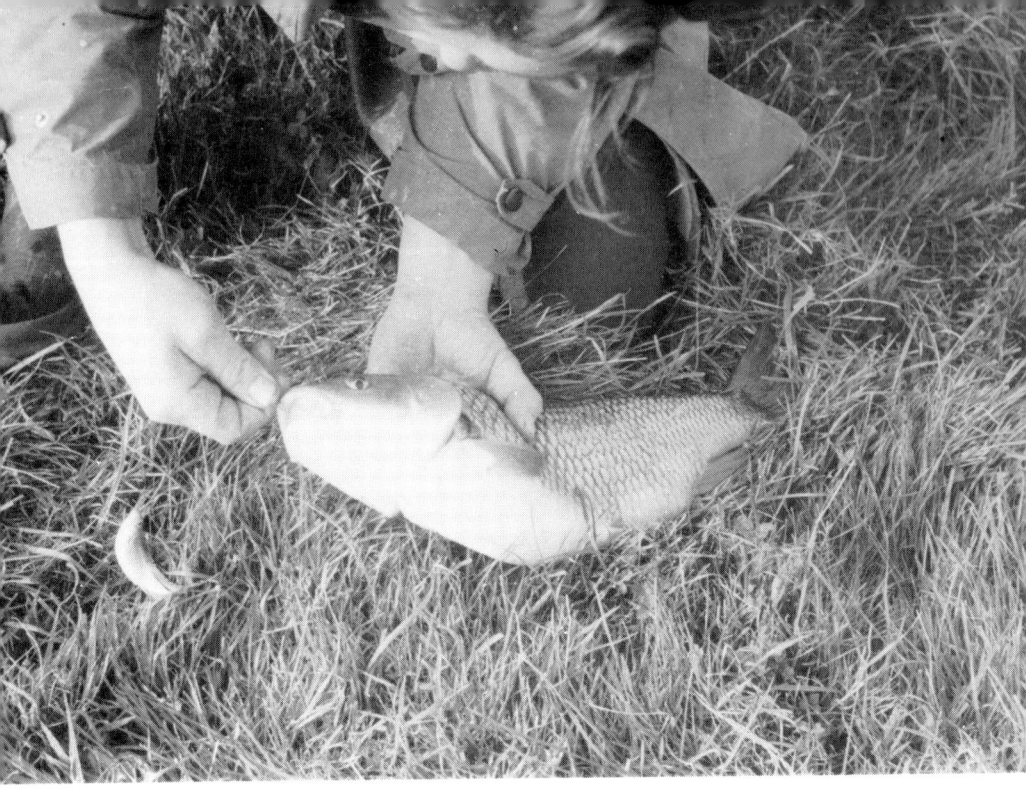

A 4¾lb chub and the bleak it took in the middle of a hot summer's day.

The subject of high protein bait is much too vast to discuss here and for those interested I recommend reading what Kevin Maddocks has to say in his book 'Carp Fever'.

One of the oldest—and deadliest—chub baits is cheesepaste. I almost said 'cheese' but some brands are not recommended because of their tendency to harden quickly in water, especially in winter. (Cream cheeses, at least those I have tried, are especially bad.) While this applies to most cheeses some harden more quickly than others. Because of this I mix my cheeses with breadpaste which remains soft although in extreme temperatures (40°F and under) it often requires further kneading throughout the day to ensure it remains soft—which is very important. Although chub will pick up hard cheese and eat it, difficulty will be experienced pulling the hook out from the cheese and into the chub's mouth. At *all* times cheese (and cheesepaste) must be soft—so soft it will not withstand being retrieved.

During the 60's I was a keen match angler and one day fished a match on the river Thame. It was January and very cold with the river frozen over apart from a channel 3ft wide running down the centre. The match was a 'rover' and the angler immediately below me kept striking but not catching anything. Interested (because I had had no cause to strike!) I went to see what was going on. As I watched, his rod top pulled round in an almighty curve, he struck and missed. "I've had enough of this", he said, "Can't hit 'em—I'm off", and gathering up his tackle he moved. Seconds later I had too—into his vacated swim! He had, I noticed, been using cheese which was still on his hook when he retrieved and I needed no reminding that his bait was too hard—the reason for those thumping bites and continual misses.

Moving my lead to within three inches of the hook I cast a small piece of crust into the ice-free channel, holding the line between my fingers and watching the rod top closely. Minutes later the rod top moved forward half an inch—no more—but half an inch was enough; chub number one.

In less than two hours I landed five chub from five bites including a four-pounder and won the match with pounds to spare! All my bites that day were minute but because the bait was soft the chub hung on and swallowed it and were easy to hook. The angler who presented me with the opportunity was using cheese which was far too hard— also a weight which was far too heavy, another factor not in his favour. The chub picked up his bait, moved off, felt the weight and bolted, with the cheese only on the edge of their lips. The angler's response to the rod bending over pulled cheese from the chub's mouth with the hook still inside the bait. That is but one example; I could quote others but the rule is always the same: never use too much weight, and when using cheese or cheesepaste make sure it is soft and will not harden in the water.

My favourite (I'm not sure about the chub) is Danish Blue which besides being soft has quite a strong smell, another factor chub fishermen should remember. The longer you keep cheesepaste the better chub like it. I keep mine two weeks before using it and after four weeks any remaining is really 'high'.

For many years my regular fishing companion gladly accepted any cheesepaste of mine which had become too 'high' for my comfort, on which he caught a lot of chub. Many successful chub anglers rate Gorgonzola very highly (no pun intended) but I cannot stand the smell. Of one thing I am certain: anyone lacking a sense of smell could, other factors being equal, become the greatest chub-catcher of all time.

The author being filmed by BBC Television catching chub from a Thames tributary.

All this means therefore that the mixing of cheesepaste is very important. Anglers have their own methods but here is mine which has stood me in good stead ever since I first used cheesepaste over 40 years ago. First, get a loaf three days old at least, cut the crusts off and cut the loaf into slices about an inch thick. Each slice is then held under a tap or dipped in water for a few seconds. It is then placed into the palm of one hand and kneaded with the thumb of the other hand. This is done over a clean bowl. If the bread is sufficiently old, with the correct amount of water added, it should crumble while being kneaded, with crumbs falling into the bowl. These are picked out at intervals and mixed in. Do each slice in turn and then put all the lumps together. This is then kneaded until the paste is soft with *no* lumps (chub reject lumpy paste very quickly).

Past writers advised mixing paste in a clean rag but that is not necessary providing your hands are clean—which applies to anything likely to come into contact with the paste. Failure to use old bread will mean a doughy, lumpy, grey-coloured paste. Good paste cannot be made from new bread; this must always be remembered. Now get the cheese—old or new, it doesn't matter. If old it should be grated on a nutmeg grater; if new (which I prefer) it is simply kneaded like the paste then, when ready, it is kneaded into the paste. When finished the paste should be kept in a plastic bait box and if necessary kneaded to the right consistency immediately before fishing.

Much has been written about scented baits. Oil of Rodium, and aniseed, are just two of many oils some anglers say improve their catches. To which I say "cobblers"! Of course you will catch chub on paste with oil(s) added—I have many times—and although there is no doubt chub approve of the smell of cheese and other additives, presentation is far, far more important. A badly-presented piece of paste with a 'wonder oil' added is no substitute for poor presentation.

Having said that I firmly believe some anglers can improve their chances by adding oil(s) to their hookbait and if this appears to be a contradiction of what I have just said let me assure you it is not, and hereby hangs a tale.

A companion of mine could never catch fish on plain breadpaste. One day I was pulling out roach one after the other while he, fishing alongside, was struggling (but not with fish). I gave him some of my unscented paste, but still he caught nothing, and being interested I baited his hook for him and bingo—a roach. I placed another piece on his hook—another roach. Then he baited his hook with my paste— nothing. Throughout that afternoon if I baited his hook he caught; when he baited—no bites. Then the penny dropped; my companion I knew sweated a great deal whereas I did not. Was the sweat from his fingers, I wondered, tainting the paste and deterring the roach from taking it? Another thing: his favourite bait was cheesepaste on which he caught chub and roach, and I wondered whether the smell of his cheesepaste (which was always 'high') counteracted the human taint. It may not have done, but I firmly believe his failure over many years we fished together to catch fish on plain breadpaste was due to his sweaty hands, sweat which made no difference when his paste contained a stronger cheese smell to counteract it. For anglers who sweat unduly, the addition of oil in paste could well prove a vital factor— but only for that reason.

When I was at school and while in my 'teens' I spent many hours along the Thames fly fishing. In those days boat traffic was light, weed growth prolific and the water very much clearer than it is today. My main quarry was chub and over the years many around three pounds graced my net. My range of flies was limited to around six with a Zulu—a black hackled fly and red wool tag—the favourite. To watch the fly coming downstream, then a pair of white lips closing over it was exciting fishing and during those years I learnt much about chub behaviour. Such days have, however, long since passed, with heavy boat traffic and coloured water rendering fly fishing a waste of time. Yet, despite the deterioration of our rivers and streams, a few remain where chub can still be tempted with a fly, but my reason for mentioning this is that on some gravel pits opportunities exist where I firmly believe some very big chub can be taken on fly.

One summer evening on a pit some 100 yards from the bank Geoff Barnes and I noticed some large bow-waves and closer observation revealed a hatch of sedges — on which the chub were obviously feeding. Since then, similar experiences have occurred on other pits and although I have not attempted to catch stillwater chub on flies there is, I think, little doubt it can be done.

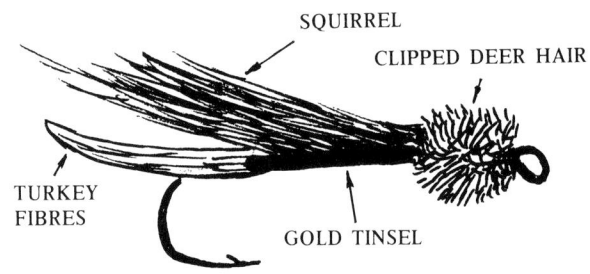

MUDDLER MINNOW
HOOK 6 OR 8

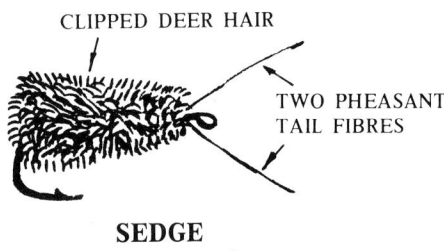

SEDGE
HOOK 6 OR 8

FIG 4

Being a trout angler I catch a lot of trout on 'Muddler Minnows' stripped back fast on a floating line when there is a chop on the water. The action produces a bow-wave behind the 'Muddler' which trout find most attractive and which I believe chub would too. Without getting too technical a 'Muddler Minnow' consists of several bunches of deer hair whipped to, say, a number 6 hook with a tail of turkey feather fibres and a turkey wing over a bunch of squirrel hair. The deer hair after being whipped is clipped off close to the hook leaving you with a very buoyant fly. Similar patterns but consisting of only the deer hair with two long antennae meant to represent a sedge are also very good.

The tactics which I suggest — and which I intend putting into practice — are these. Attached to a 4lb b.s. point on a floating line with the wind blowing from behind, the fly would be floated out to where chub could be seen or where they might be. Dusk and dawn excepted, observations suggest long casting would be necessary and you would certainly need a ruffled surface to hide the nylon. Unlike when trouting, I suggest not stripping the 'Muddler' back but allowing it to float around giving it an occasional twitch to impart 'life' to it.

Over the years I have taken many chub on spinners, another branch of chub fishing sadly neglected by chub specialists, including me! Why this should be I don't know (in my case it is time), but like the 'Muddler' it is well worth persevering with. In one gravel pit the chub are particularly difficult to catch, most days remaining well out from the bank, beating a hasty retreat on the rare occasions you do see one lying in the margins. One day a young lad approached me with a chub. On the top of its head was a strawberry-looking object the size of a man's thumb — the reason why the lad had brought the chub to show me. I could offer no explanation but asked him what he had caught it on. "A kidney spoon", was the reply. Having caught plenty of chub on kidney spoons that did not surprise me; what was surprising was that he had caught the chub at all! And by the look of his rod (about 8ft) and a half-filled spool, not far out from the bank either.

Later that morning I heard a shout and found the lad playing another: two chub in less than an hour on a water where you are lucky to catch two in a season! Admittedly it was autumn, a time when chub become pre-occupied with fry, a time too when small spinners and plugs might prove the downfall of many chub.

One afternoon I was fishing another pit when an angler caught a chub of some 5lbs on a jointed plug intended for pike. Although one

swallow does not make a summer on a water which gives up its chub grudgingly and then mostly at night, to catch one in daylight on a plug close in encouraged me to try plugs at night, and although at the time of writing it has not proved successful it is, I think, only a matter of time . . .

In weirpools in summer, chub take minnows greedily and I have just acquired a range of Rapala plugs which I intend giving an extended trial. Anyone interested in plug fishing for chub could do much worse than take a look at the Rapala range for it is, I think, only a matter of time before an enormous chub is taken by this very neglected branch of chub fishing.

I don't normally write about something I have little experience of but the 'Muddler Minnow', spinners and plugs are exceptions to my rule. Both methods are, I believe, worthy of consideration, particularly in stillwaters and I intend finding out more about them. For starters I recommend: flies; (dry) Zulu, Crane Fly (Daddy Longlegs); Sedges (made from deerhair); Muddler Minnow. Spinners: Fly spoons; Vibros. Plugs: Rapalas; any small one-jointed patterns.

The chub with a 'strawberry' on its nose.

A big chub lying in the margins.

4. Location

Where rivers and streams are concerned, chub are likely to be found anywhere and it would take less space to say where chub may not be than where. Having said that, there are places which chub prefer and which, with experience, are apparent at a glance.

Obvious holding places are 'rafts' of rubbish, overhanging trees, bulrushes, bridge supports, under water lilies (cabbages), sharp bends, vertical banks — especially clay ones — weir pools, where there is a sudden change in current speed, ranunculus (streamer weed), ledges, and fast water in the middle of the river. Fast water, especially if several yards out from the bank, is often ignored by anglers who believe, wrongly, that fish cannot hold position. But think: how many times have you in flood water seen small fish like bleak dimpling in the middle of the river in water where even 2oz of lead will not hold bottom? This is a common occurrence, and if bleak can hold position other fish can too. Never ignore fast water; only when it is too fast to fish properly should it be passed by.

In summer and autumn, chub can be located by scattering large pieces of crust on the surface then waiting for a piece to be attacked or eaten. At such times, floating crust usually proves successful (obviously!); sometimes though, for reasons I cannot understand, it isn't, but bread fished at mid-water under a float, or in fairly shallow water a bait on the bottom is better.

In small rivers and streams, location by floating crust often works in winter too. What must be remembered however is the chub may not want floating crust at that particular time (or the crust may be travelling too fast for it) but at least you know one is present — and most times others too. If uncertain whether chub are present and there are few, if any, holding places, fishing different swims for, say, twenty minutes at a time will usually produce a fish or two. This way many chub have been caught from swims which looked most un-chubby but where there was obviously something, not apparent to me, which held them.

Sometimes, even in an obvious holding spot, bites will occur in a very small area although it all looks alike. One example was the 'Two Willows' swim on Dick Walker's reach of the Ouse before the dredger reared its ugly bucket. As its name implies, there were two willow trees (on the opposite bank) a few feet apart, their roots reaching down into the water—the obvious place to put a bait. But the chub thought differently; between the two willows and in midstream was a small patch of clean gravel (visible only in summer with the sun overhead) and it was on that small patch of gravel your bait had to be: not once can I recall a bite occurring anywhere else in that swim.

In stillwaters, location is much more difficult, especially in those where the chub rarely show themselves—on the bank or otherwise. Here is it a question of getting to know the water, with early morning and late evenings in summer the most likely time to see any. At such times, crust scattered on the surface often provides a give-away as to the areas the chub frequent; likewise concentrations of fry. Here, chub are never very far away especially when the fry are present over a long period such as in autumn and close to weedbeds.

Although chub are often seen in gravel pits during the day, cruising or bow-waving on the surface, I don't think those areas are necessarily those they frequent most. A walk around stillwaters at first light often results in chub being seen, especially in the margins. In stillwaters—at least those I fish—chub patrol the margins regularly at night (see chapter 7) and the angler who takes up position at dusk where chub have been seen in early morning, stands a good chance of catching one during the hours of darkness. But whether you fish at night or not, the fact that chub frequent these areas is enough and plans can be formulated to catch them.

Stillwaters excepted, locating chub is not too difficult once you know the features to look for, but you should try fishing featureless swims also.

5. Rivers

Legering

In recent years anglers, particularly match anglers, have enjoyed enormous success legering casters, hemp and maggots on fine tackle —2lb lines, 1lb bottoms, 18-24 hooks. This 'new' technique described later in this chapter has resulted not only in some remarkable catches but big chub too. Unfortunately, many of the younger anglers, having 'grown up' with the technique, tend to ignore legering (including touch legering) with bread, cheesepaste, meat, worms, etc., which is a pity because it remains a fine method which still brings me a lot of fish — and will hopefully bring me a great many more.

Before I discuss baits, terminal rigs, etc., I will give a brief mention of 'downstream and across' legering because if this is not understood — worse still, not practised — much good fishing time will be wasted. In my early legering days I missed a lot of 'good' bites which I could not understand. Note that I say 'good' bites because many of these resulted in the rod top pulling round as much as two feet, but even if it didn't move that far, whatever it did there was no mistaking that it had moved! The missed bites bothered me but not, as it turned out, for very long.

Around the time I was putting my legering together I started trout fishing with the wet fly on the river Windrush. The books advised casting downstream and retrieving with the fly at right angles to the rod. On my first trip I got bites—vicious bites—the majority of which, however, I missed. And I didn't like missing fish— especially trout!

Determined to put a stop to such nonsense, on my next visit I decided to try casting upstream so, as the fly travelled downstream, there was a bow in the line. Immediately the previous fast pulls turned into slow ones—pulls I had no trouble hooking—as many

42 FISHING FOR BIG CHUB

These came from the Upper Thames in successive casts—5lbs 1oz, 4lbs 12ozs and 4lbs 4oz.

trout found to their cost. That a bow in the line should make such a difference made me think, and the next time I went coarse fishing I tried casting across and slightly upstream so, like the fly, the lead and bait rolled along the bottom with a bow in the line. To my delight the once-vicious, almost unhittable, bites turned into very small bites often difficult to see but once I knew what to look for they were unmistakeable, and—important this—*very* easy to hook.

Since then, when discussing legering problems, I have stressed the importance of a bow in the line. The effect of the bow is that when a fish pulls it pulls not against the rod top but the line which 'cushions' the pull and which in turn encourages the fish to hang on to the bait. When it feels the rod top a chub usually bolts, at the same time spitting out the bait. By the time the angler strikes—even if it is only a split second after—the chub has spat out the bait, hence the missed bite and areas of blue air surrounding the angler.

When legering in fairly wide rivers—rivers wide enough, that is, to permit a bow in the line—my favourite baits are crust, cheesepaste, sausage and luncheon meat, in that order. In winter when bites are often 'small' and finicky, pieces of crust $3/8$ in square are often best. During prolonged cold spells however, large pieces of bread and cheesepaste—large enough to cover a number 4 hook—are often taken; during the 1962/63 freeze-up I caught a lot of chub on large baits fished alongside thick ice in water temperatures under 40°F.

During mild spells, in summer and autumn too, pieces 1in square, cheesepaste and sausage meat the size of a walnut, or cubes of luncheon meat $1/2$ in square are often preferred.

The type of bottom must also be considered: over a gravelly or weedless one, cheesepaste and sausage meat on a 15in tail is my choice; over a weedy bottom, crust on a 6in tail. In weirpools with snaggy bottoms (and few haven't) I prefer crust which keeps the hook clear; also where a bait is more likely to tickle the chub's palate if fished stationary. But whatever the bait, one thing is certain: some days, some bites will pass unnoticed, so knowing what to look for is very important indeed.

In situations where the bait is required to roll along the bottom, the first essential is to make sure the amount of weight being used is such that it will *not quite* hold bottom. The action on the rod top will tell whether it is right or not. The tip should move forward and hold still for about a minute, then jerk back a couple of times before pulling round, but only slightly, again.

Now bites: there is a wide difference of opinion as to how a chub bite registers, the usual advice being to wait until the top pulls over. I state quite emphatically: *ignore* such advice. Bites from chub vary but the most common ones are these: the rod will move forward an inch or two and remain there; it may suddenly 'kick back', remaining in that position; it may pull forward four or five inches; it may suddenly move back and forwards as if the current has moved the lead, or it may pull forward quickly an inch followed almost immediately by a pull of up to four inches.

The first three bites should be struck immediately and will, most times, result in the fish being hooked. The bite similar to the current moving the lead is also a confident one although many anglers think it is the current and do nothing. With experience you can tell the difference, but I can't explain it on paper. All I *can* say is that the initial 'kick-back' is slightly 'sharper' than when the current is responsible.

Should the strike be delayed with this bite, the chub is often hooked well down with the possibility of the hook being bitten off by its pharyngeal (throat) teeth. The sharp 'jab' followed immediately by a pull is another 'sitter', but don't strike on the 'jab'.

What *must* be remembered is that bites are often difficult to detect especially in a wind. The golden rule, as always, is—if in doubt, strike. This applies to any suspicious movement. Over the years I have caught countless numbers of chub by striking because I was not sure whether the rod top moved or not. In a wind the rod top, no matter how still you hold the rod, will move about, although slightly, but suddenly the movement, small though it may be, is 'different'. Don't sit there thinking "was that a bite or not"—strike, if it wasn't you have only lost a bit of bait.

Now groundbait. When fishing with bread or cheesepaste I use soaked breadcrumbs mixed to a consistency so the balls do not break up until they reach bottom. The mixing is of course important, the reason why I always take my breadcrumbs dry, mixing at the waterside after I have made a close study of the current speed.

For starters, I introduce two orange-size balls after I have made a trial cast (without hookbait) to ascertain the area my hookbait will cover or, if fishing a stationary bait, exactly where I shall anchor it. If and when a bite occurs, another ball is introduced and, should bites continue, further one-ball introductions at about fifteen minute intervals. This is of course only a rough guide; if bites are coming quickly and you think it is unlikely you can overfeed, the number of balls can be increased.

Although I have mentioned 'orange-size balls' this does not always apply and certainly not in small rivers less than, say, ten yards across. While an orange-size ball of soaked breadcrumbs thrown into a river like the Thames will not disturb a shoal, a similar-sized ball in a narrow river or stream will not do your chances any good at all! In small streams I reduce the size to that of a chicken's egg, sometimes smaller still, especially on cold days in winter in low water temperatures. On such days when a piece of crust fished stationary is more likely to succeed, I introduce very little breadcrumb and then only occasionally.

This near five-pounder was the result of striking at a movement hardly discernable on the quiver tip.

Now days when a stationary bait is best. Here the amount of weight must be such that it will hold bottom but *only just*, for at all times immediately a chub picks up the bait the lead *must* move; if it doesn't many bites will pass unnoticed. Bites, however, will often be small and difficult to detect, but if they are seen, easy to hook.

One winter I was invited to fish a reach of the Upper Ouse I had never fished before. I was the guest of Fred J. Taylor's brother Joe, one of the finest chub fishermen I have ever fished with, and I knew that anything Joe told me had to be treated with the utmost respect.

At that time I had never caught a 5lb chub but the reach I was fishing—which Joe knew like the back of his hand—held a few and I was confident of catching my first 'five'. I arrived in a snowstorm—in my experience a time when chub often feed ravenously—and Joe eventually put me in a swim with the remark, "If you catch one here it will be five pounds".

The hotspot was several yards downstream against the far bank and Joe said that a stationary bait was essential. Two trial casts showed I had judged the weight correctly and after placing a small piece of crust on the hook I cast to the spot, tightened to the lead, then, holding the rod and line, sat down to await developments.

The tip of my rod was bent slightly over by the current pull on the line when it suddenly kicked back half an inch—no more—and stayed there. The strike resulted in line being stripped from the spool and shortly after a chub, two ounces short of five pounds, was wallowing in the net. Joe was a little disappointed, but I was elated, not only because of the size of the chub but also because I had recognised the very tiny, yet unmistakeable, indication on the rod top.

These days when quivertips and rod rests play such a large part in legering techniques, the art—and it *is* an art—of touch legering is largely forgotten. This is a pity because while quivertips and rod rests have a vital part to play, days occur when it is far, far better to hold the rod and line. For example: it is winter and conditions dictate that a moving bait is more likely to be taken than a stationary one. Having adjusted the lead so it will just and *only* just roll bottom, you cast and immediately the lead touches bottom you take the line and with the rod held steady watch the rod top.

If you have done it right the lead will roll a few inches, stop, then seconds later move again, and so on. All this can be felt on the line but suddenly the movement is different; it is 'sharper' or more pro-

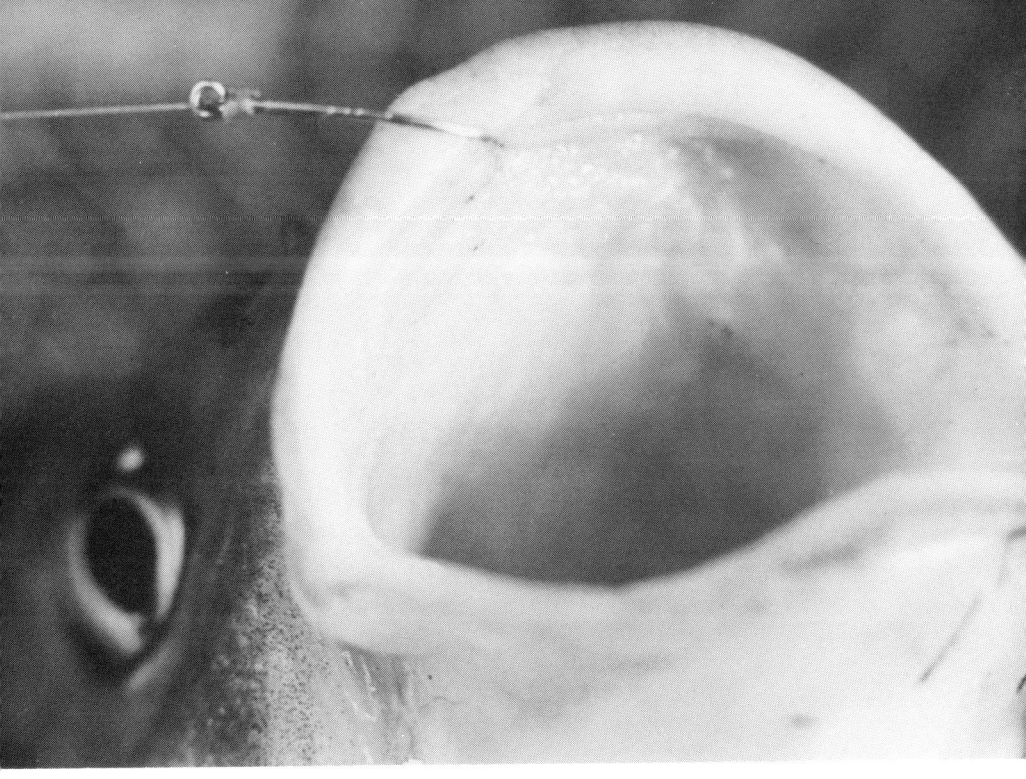

A number 6 hook looks very small in the mouth of a four pound chub.

longed. But whatever form it takes it is *different*, you strike — and bingo!

Now then: the movement which caused the chub's downfall was so minute, only in very calm conditions (and how often do you encounter those?) would it have been seen on the rod top or quiver. That is one example; now another.

You are fishing a swim where the water is shallow — five feet say — and very fast, so fast that as much line as possible must be kept clear of the water to permit good presentation. Here, the rod is pointed skywards. By placing an extra long rod rest some two feet in front of you with the rod butt on the ground you can achieve just that, but this unfortunately reduces your chances. Instead, you sit with the rod handle tucked into your groin with the rod pointing skywards and with the line between two fingers of your left hand (if you are right-handed). If you watch the rod top (which you must if the rod is supported on a rest) you will finish up asking your doctor for a prescription for neck ache, but by touch-legering you don't have to watch the rod top — and the visit to the doctor will not be necessary.

If you are holding bottom tightly but with the right amount of lead (so that when a fish picks up the bait the lead will move) the line will remain tight; by rolling the bottom the line will tighten then slacken, tighten again, and so on. At such times although some bites will result in the rod top pulling over and the line tightening in your fingers, most times it will kick back (when the line suddenly becomes slack). But when a fish causes the lead to move, the indication on the line is sharper; not much, but a little and, with practice, easily recognisable.

Days occur too when bites, although confident, demand a rapid response. With the rod in two rests even if your striking hand is close to the rod many of these bites will be missed; I speak from experience, and my reactions are *very* quick.

Initially, touch legering is, I admit, difficult but with practice will become so easy you will wonder why you did not try it before. Just *how* you hold the rod and line is a matter of preference but I do it in this way: the rod handle is tucked under my arm, my right hand (I'm right handed) gripping the rod at the reel seat with the rod supported by my knee. The line is held between thumb and first finger of my left hand. Fast water excepted, I point the rod tip at the water keeping it as close to the water as possible. Some days—when for instance it is cold or windy—I support the rod in a rest but still holding it and the line as described. This way it is easier to hold the rod still or almost so, and the more steady you hold the rod the more likely you are to see bites.

I cannot demonstrate the importance of touch legering better than to describe a favourite Thames weirpool of mine. Like all weirpools it is snaggy and in one area of some 20 yards there are boulders with a clear area of gravel ten yards long between them. Whether there are two large boulders or several small ones I don't know, but if you allow the lead to hit bottom too far up or downstream of the clear patch of gravel you don't get it back; and that small gravelly patch is a very hot, hot spot indeed.

In summer the chub do not appear to be present, taking up residence once the cold weather sets in. The trouble is, because the swim is some 20 yards from the bank and some 14ft deep it can only be fished properly when the current speed is right, i.e. not so fast that you can't hold bottom between the boulders. But catch it right and chub—big chub too—are almost guaranteed.

Having fished the pool for over twenty years I think I have it sussed out and what you do is this: after adjusting the lead(s) so it will hold bottom fairly hard (you don't want it to roll towards and into the boulders)—yet at the same time move when a chub picks up the bait —you cast to a point on the far bank and let it sink on a *slack* line when it will eventually come to rest on the clean gravel. The rod is then pointed at the water with the rod over your knee, line between the fingers. Due to the depth of water and distance from the bank you must strike at the first indication, otherwise the chub has gone. But that's not all: between the the bank and the swim are more boulders and if you strike and miss and do not hold the rod up as high as you can *immediately* and wind like mad, then two minutes later you will be groping around in your box for another terminal tackle.

Touch legering is the *only* way to fish that swim; the anglers who fish there with their rods in rests simply do not catch—to say nothing of lost leads, hooks and lengths of nylon left in those boulders.

My love of weirpools has also taught me that one of the most productive places is where few anglers cast—right in the 'white water' directly over, or just past, the sill. This is because anglers believe—understandably—that a lot of lead is necessary to hold the bait in position, only to find themselves firmly snagged in the boulders or stones. Not so; the answer is not a lot of lead but hardly any! Under the turbulent water is an undercurrent going towards the sill which, when the cast is right, will carry both lead and bait along to the pocket of steadier water and then hold it there. Getting the cast right isn't easy and initially several attempts may be necessary before you succeed. Cast so that the lead lands right against the sill *just and only just* on the outside of the turbulent water. As the lead hits the water immediately let out slack line. All being well the bait will be carried along by the under-tow. If the lead doesn't go under first time, try again. The secret is placing it correctly, then letting out line at the crucial moment.

Bites are generally decisive, the rod top either pulling over or a knock felt on the line. Hold the rod high, keeping as much line above the water as possible. Failure to do so will result in the bait and lead being pulled out of position.

I recall a bitterly cold winter's day fishing the Thames when the cold finally got the better of my fingers and I found touch legering impossible. Not far away was a little weirpool which would provide

Geoff Barnes fishing the Cherwell. Note how close his hands are kept to the rod, waiting for the smallest movement on this very cold morning.

shelter from the bitter wind, a weirpool though which rarely produced chub over 3lbs. Did I *really* want a 3lb chub, I asked myself, or should I go home? It was, I decided, one of those days when anything (well, almost anything) is welcome. I decided to give the pool a try.

Positioning myself level with the sill I pinched just one swan shot on the line and made a trial cast; yes, the single swan shot held. On the hook I placed a piece of crust and several minutes later felt a tiny pluck on the line. I knew it was a good fish long before I saw it and, at 4lb 14oz it was the biggest chub I had known to come from that pool, a fish which today seventeen years later has, to the best of my knowledge, never been beaten. A surprising and somewhat lucky fish; such is the magic of weirpools.

In chapter 2 I mention quivertips. Although I rarely roach fish without one, occasions occur when I use them for chub too — in situations where they give a definite advantage over touch legering. I'll give one example. I fish a reach of the river Windrush which holds a

Joe Taylor fishing a once 'hot' big chub swim on the Upper Ouse.

fair head of 4lb + chub and 2lb + roach. Most days fishing is difficult with few bites resulting. It is a hard water but one where the fish are big—a perfect specimen hunter's water.

Bites on this reach are not only few and far between, most days they are minute too. I don't mind that, because the river lies in a valley and is less affected by wind than other rivers I fish. Because of this, touch legering is tiring—a situation where a quivertip really scores. The rod is supported by two rests with the quiver as close to the water as possible (where it is least affected by wind) with my striking hand positioned close to the rod. Many of my four pound chub and two pound roach from the water have moved the quiver less than ½in—one 2¼lb roach moved it so little I only struck on suspicion. I have caught chub too when the movement on the quiver has been barely discernible. In situations like these, a quivertip is vital with touch legering taking a definite back seat.

Upstream legering

When legering in rivers most anglers, quite rightly, fish downstream and across. Sometimes, however, due to the nature of the swim and the position from where you are obliged to sit, it is not always possible to do this. Dense weed, bankside trees, bushes, and other factors, often determine this where there is only one thing you can do — you leger upstream.

Upstream legering has several advantages, one being that because you are downstream of the fish it is much less likely to see you. Some anglers find the method difficult mainly I think because it entails holding the rod and watching and feeling for bites. Quivertips and swingtips have no part to play in upstream legering, a method however which, once understood, is very deadly indeed.

First I will describe a swim in which there is a dense patch of ranunculus and where the fish are lying under it or on the edge. On a sliding link you place sufficient weight to hold bottom but *only just* — that is *very* important. The link is stopped some 3-4ft from the hook and although this length of tail is not critical it should not be less than 30ins. With an overhead cast, the lead lands just upstream of the weed and level with its outside edge. As it hits bottom, take up the slack and hold the rod high with as much line as possible out of the water, the line between two fingers. Although you can leger sitting down it is much better to stand.

When a chub picks up the bait it will invariably move downstream at the same time moving the lead, resulting in the line falling slack. Because of this, when the strike is made the rod is brought back well over the shoulder. (Sometimes a second strike will be necessary, the angler at the same time stepping backwards.) Most bites consist of the line falling slack although occasionally the fish will move upstream, the line tightening and the rod top pulling over.

I have stressed the importance of the lead being such that it will *only just* hold bottom although sometimes current pull or weed touching the line will cause the lead to move, resulting in false bites. With experience the difference between a false bite and a proper one is very noticeable, the latter causing the line to fall just that bit sharper than when current pull or weed is responsible.

When legering upstream alongside ranunculus the bait should be as close to the weed as possible—which means accurate casting. In summer chub lie right under the weed, rarely emerging from it, and it is vital that your bait is under the weed—hence the long tail. Sometimes a dense patch of weed will be encountered which cannot be fished from down or upstream. Here, providing the weed patch is no wider than the length of the rod, it can be fished across stream. Take up position halfway or thereabouts along the weed and tackle up as for upstream legering. The lead should land *just* outside the weed and slightly upstream of you, then as it hits bottom the slack line is taken up.

By keeping the rod well up, the lead will slowly trundle along the bottom, the rod top bouncing back and forth as it does so, the line at the same time bowed and dropping downstream. Bites are determined by the bow in the line increasing rapidly and/or the bounces on the rod top being sharper. Sometimes the weed wavering in the current will move outwards and back again touching the line as it does so, causing the rod top to pull over and/or the line to move downstream. Here, bites are more difficult to determine although with experience you learn to tell the difference between the weed and fish.

When a chub is hooked the fun really starts, it being impossible to land the fish from where you are standing. (As with upstream legering it is better to stand up—the weed will hide you from the fish.) Prior to fishing, place the landing net downstream and where the weed patch ends. Immediately a chub is hooked walk downstream, at the same time keeping the rod held high and well out from you until the netting position is reached. Somewhat 'hairy' fishing, especially when the weed is very dense and the chub big. Exciting though—and *very* effective!

Legering casters/maggots on fine tackle

Later in this chapter I describe the effectiveness of hemp/caster/ bronze maggot fished on fine tackle under a float, but you don't have to use a float to fish these small baits on fine tackle; they can be presented on leger tackle too. As with the float, initially I had fears about the method, not least of all the question of striking without breaking. But I was surprised, for providing care is taken and the strike controlled it is surprising just what a 2lb line and 1lb b.s.

bottom can take. Another thing: when float fishing you have a split second longer to remember what you are doing but when the rod top or quiver moves—especially when it has not moved for some time—your reaction is instantaneous. This may not apply to all anglers of course—some are much more controlled than others; nevertheless, 'Mr Average' will react just that little bit quicker, and where striking is concerned I'm one of the 'Mr Averages'!

The secret lies mainly in the rod, which must have a soft action. Poky, stiff-actioned rods increase the chances of breaking but a soft-actioned rod cushions the strike—even when your response is harder than it need have been. A friend uses a modified fly rod and other factors being equal there is much sense in that. Although you can use a simple link leger, a blockend feeder, although not essential, is nevertheless desirable. Whether you use an open-ended feeder (more of that later) depends largely what you intend putting inside, but for starters I will discuss the use of a conventional blockend feeder.

Whether the feeder is allowed to slide along or is fixed to the line is a matter of preference; I think it matters little. Having used both methods I prefer the former. Both set-ups are illustrated. Most times—to start with anyway—a tail of about 18-20in is about right. This, however, may have to be shortened or lengthened if the presentation is not right or if bites prove difficult to hit.

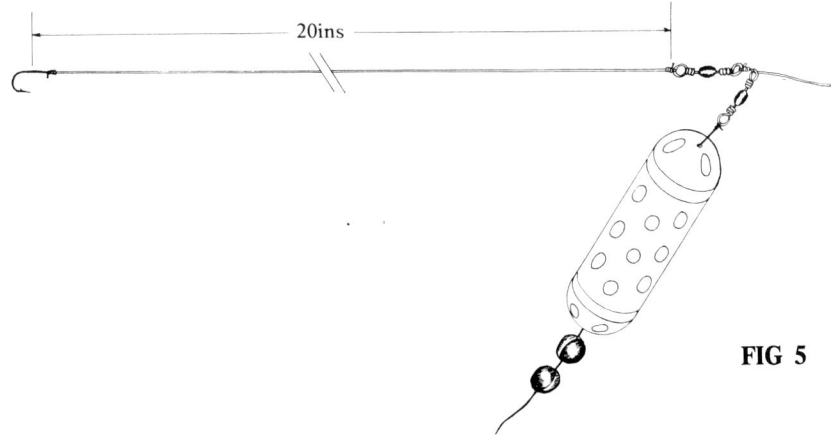

FIG 5

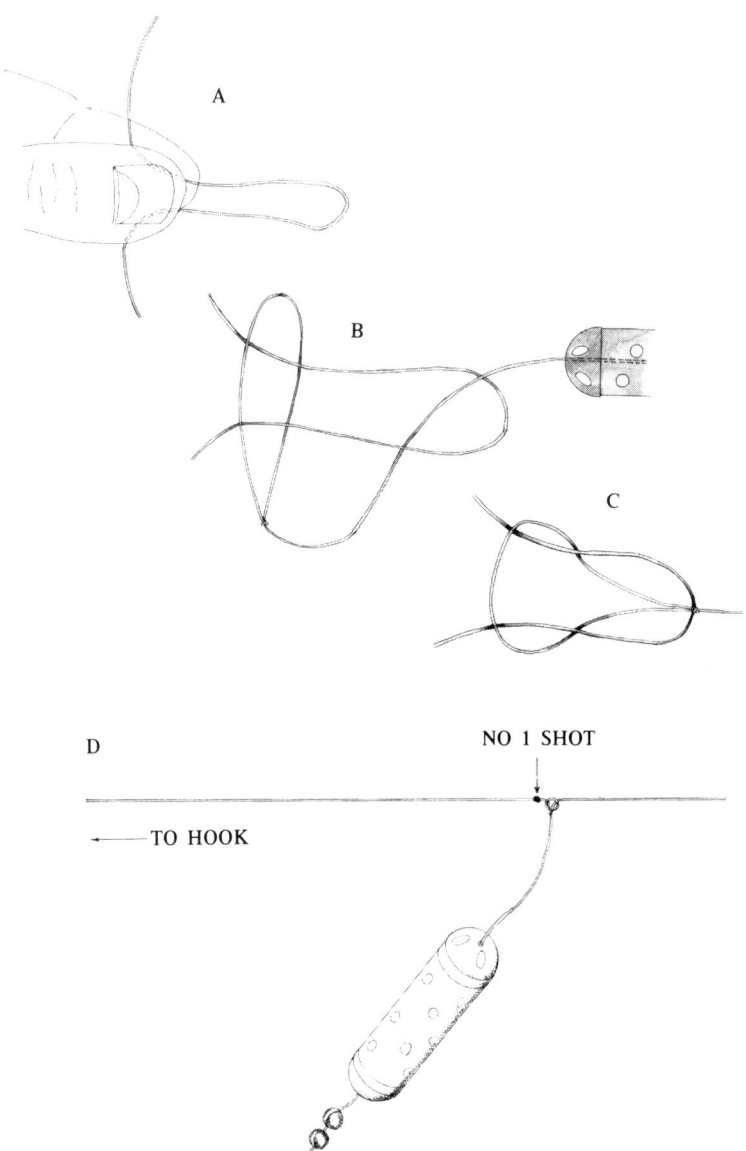

A. FOLD MAIN LINE INTO LOOP BETWEEN THUMB AND FINGER.
B. TAKE LOOP OF NYLON ATTACHED TO FEEDER AND THREAD THROUGH LOOP IN MAIN LINE.
C. PULL BOTH LOOPS TIGHTLY TOGETHER.
D. FEEDER ATTACHED TO MAIN LINE.

Some days the chub will not be feeding on or close to the bottom but, say, 4ft above. If therefore you are fairly certain chub are present but bites are not forthcoming or only rarely, try increasing the tail to 3ft, but remember: with a long tail, bites are sometimes difficult to see and the first indication you have is when you reel in and find the caster(s) shelled or the maggot(s) sucked. This means you are not seeing the bites quickly enough (by this I mean you saw a bite and missed only to find the bait shelled or sucked) or, worse still, not seeing them at all. The short answer is to change to float tackle, but this is not always possible, so reduce the tail to about 8ins. Should a chub result your next job is to get the chub feeding closer to the bottom and by using a short tail most days they will.

When casting, I allow the feeder to fall through the water on a *tight* line with my eyes glued firmly to the quiver or rod top. Get chub going and they will often intercept the feeder and hookbait as they drop through the water or immediately they touch bottom. Always cast so the feeder as it swings and drops towards you empties most of the contents over the swim. The distance you over cast is determined by the depth of the swim.

Now bites: as the feeder sinks watch for the bite which results in the line falling rapidly towards you—or faster than it should. Other bites will take the form of kick-backs, a gentle rocking back and forth of the tip or pulls varying between 6ins and 2ft. Some days you will require eyes like a hawk; on others the chub almost hook themselves.

When using casters or bronze maggots in a feeder I prefer the conventional Feederlink. For hemp, either neat, or hemp/cereal and caster/cereal, I use a modified feeder. The removable cap is dispensed with and the feeder turned upside down (see Fig 6). Care must be taken to get the consistency of the cereal right—soft enough, that is, so it begins to emerge from the feeder seconds after touching bottom. When bites are not forthcoming or you can't hook them consistently, experiment. Some days two casters (or maggots) are preferred; on others just one (why such a hungry creature like chub should prefer just one caster or maggot completely baffles me). Days occur when, although a swim may be full of chub, bites only occur when the feeder is cast into a very confined area. The creation of hotspots—or rather, hot, hotspots—is a common occurrence when block-ending, where as in other forms of fishing accurate casting is essential.

FIG 6

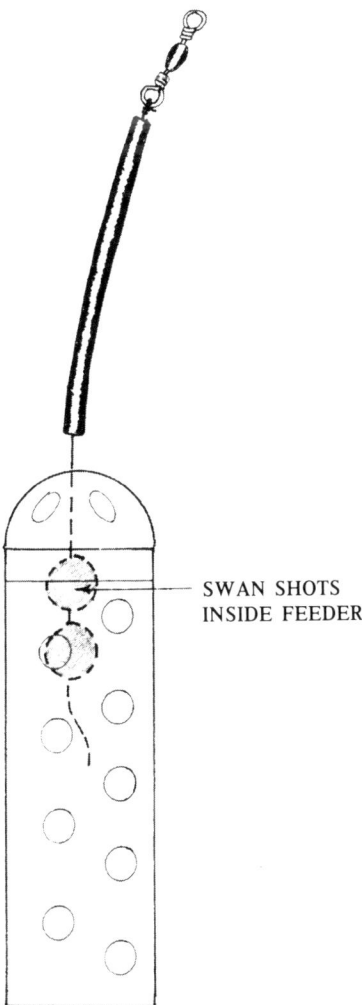

SWAN SHOTS INSIDE FEEDER

One final point—striking. 'Strike' is actually a mis-nomer, for to strike in the accepted sense will, despite a soft-actioned rod, result in breakages. The strike is more of a pull—better a pull of 6ft than a strike of 2ft. At all times the striking hand should be kept close to, or better still on, the rod. When fishing without a quiver I like to hold the rod, watching and feeling for bites.

Float fishing

Bordering the Thames a few miles above Oxford are two fields which at one time I fished a great deal. In one, a line of bulrushes some 40ft in length line the far bank with 12ft of water immediately in front of the rushes, and in that deep water lie big chub. For over ten years I fished in those fields regularly and more times than not in summer and autumn I made straight for the bulrushes. Most sessions produced at least two chub, a good one five or six. But numbers were immaterial, it was the average size of the chub that mattered. For the bulrush swim was an exceptional one for the Thames, a swim where four-pounders were the rule rather than the exception. Most days if I caught three chub one was certain to top four pounds.

But that was not all: that swim taught me a lot about chub—their habits and how deadly trotting with bread can be. When fishing other rivers and other reaches of the Thames I have applied tactics I have used in the bulrush swim to those too, tactics which have consistently produced four-pound chub and the occasional 'five'—and a smile on my face.

The river at the bulrush swim is some 25 yards wide which, plus the depth of water, meant that legering was usually impossible in winter, for in order to nobble those chub the bait had to be right against the rushes; 3ft out was no good. It was mainly a summer and autumn swim where trotting was *the* method and where legering was virtually a waste of time. The swim could only be fished properly when the wind was blowing either from the east or south: a facing westerly made accurate casting (which was essential) difficult, and correct presentation impossible, while a northerly (a downstreamer) pushed the float along too fast. But when I found an easterly or southerly wind blowing I was in business—four-pound business!

My rod was a 13ft glass model (today I use carbon), line 3lb, hook Goldstrike number 8, float a Pete Drennan 'Trotter' with a shot loading of two or three swan shots. These were bunched about 15ins from the hook. The final job was to grease the line because it *had* to float— that was very important. Upon arrival I introduced two handfuls of soaked breadcrumbs, throwing them upstream of the rushes so, unless a chub intercepted them beforehand (which was likely), they would reach bottom about halfway along the rushes. Bait was either crust or flake and I invariably commenced operations by setting the float at 10ft.

The secret of the swim was accurate casting—and I mean accurate for the float *had* to land no more than 3ft away from the rushes. To ensure the bait upon landing was directly under the float, I cast high, checking the line at the right moment then, as the lead hit the water, releasing the line so the float landed 'on top' of the lead. Being heavy, the float cocked immediately which was also important because sometimes the bait was intercepted as it was sinking.

Most times one of four indications could be expected: sometimes the float would rise upwards an inch (when the chub had taken the bait then risen in the water slightly, lifting the shots); sometimes it would travel downstream slightly faster than it should without lifting or dipping (when the chub had retained the same level in the water and was swimming downstream); sometimes it would 'pop up' an inch (I don't know what the chub was doing then but definitely rising in the water), or it would simply disappear (when I assume after taking the bait the chub continued diving towards the bottom). But the type of bait didn't matter; whatever form it took—and I say this with all modesty—I invariably hooked it; and that did matter. Providing the line floated and there was little slack on the water, misses were rare indeed.

The first time I fished the swim I lost a few chub by not giving them sufficient 'stick' immediately the hook went home and allowing them to get their noses against the rushes—and when a chub gets its nose against something the only thing you are left fighting is that 'something'! But I missed very few after that although my method was rather unorthodox. Immediately I felt the chub I took four or five steps backwards with my finger tightly on the spool (I always fished standing up). By the time the chub had realised what was going on it was too far away from the rushes to reach them and the rest was easy. When trotting the far bank of a river wider than, say, 20 yards I always stand, and unless there is something immediately behind me to prevent it I do the backward walk immediately I hook the fish. Unorthodox?—maybe; effective—definitely!

One day I could not get a bite and that puzzled me. Pulling the float down 3ft I tried again—still no bites, so I pulled it down further until I was eventually fishing at less than mid-water. If the chub were laughing when I started, they were not when I finished; what is more, the same tactics proved successful on other visits too. So remember: if bites are not forthcoming, experiment with different depths. Funny,

though, why 'chavender' should feed at different levels in a swim so often devoid of any current, but they do.

Another thing: I could invariably tell seconds after hooking a chub whether it was four pounds or not. As I stepped back and for a second or two after, if no 'thumps' occurred on the line that fish was four pounds; a 'thump', just one, and it was under. Heaven only knows how many chub between four pounds and four pounds fourteen ounces I took from the bulrush swim during the years I fished there yet strangely, I only nobbled one 'five'. The day after, I sent the film for processing and that was the last I saw of it. The processor said he was sorry and sent another film for compensation. I thanked him and said I would go and catch it again . . .

When trotting, I much prefer to fish the far bank because the rest of the shoal I find are scared much less by the disturbance — another reason why I like to hustle a fish out of the swim within seconds of hooking it — something which the stepping backward technique achieves very well.

Circumstances don't always render fishing the far bank possible but I'm never completely happy when long-trotting under my own bank. And where snags are present — and big chub are never far from them — these problems are increased. Hook a big chub at, say, 20 yards under your own bank and the chances are it will take you into a snag within seconds of being hooked. This can be partly overcome by using a very long rod — 14ft say — and pointing it at arm's length immediately the fish is hooked; nevertheless, I avoid long range trotting under my bank whenever possible.

I mentioned earlier Pete Drennan's 'Chub Trotters'. Some years later Pete discontinued the range, replacing them with 'Loaders'. Like the 'Trotter', the 'Loader' is heavy for its length with a stout tip — an essential feature of a float for trotting bread at distance. Being short and with a sensible shot-loading capacity (there are several sizes), the 'Loader' casts well and is easily seen at a distance even when only an inch, often less, is above the surface. Most times there should not be more than an inch anyway.

Despite the effectiveness of the caster/bronze maggot/fine tackle technique which has become so popular, trotted bread remains a fine

The result of a remarkable hour's fishing on the Thames; total bag 30lbs, best fish 5lb 1oz.

method and one of my favourites. Watching a float travelling downstream with a 'pop-up', slowly-travelling-downstream or crash-bang-wallop bites likely at any second is exciting fishing. And when I step backwards with one finger on the spool and feel a heavy weight but no 'thumps', my heart beats just that little bit faster with another four-pounder destined for my keepnet!

Casters and Waggler

During the 70's a method became popular on which large catches of chub were taken far in excess of anything previously known on the rivers concerned. My home river, the Thames, was one such river where catches of 30-40 chub at a sitting were taken, catches which 'bread and cheese' men like me had never experienced. Not only were some big catches taken, but big chub too, many in excess of four pounds.

The method involved the use of fine lines (2lb b.s.), 1-1½lb bottoms, and 16-24 hooks. Bait was casters fished under a 'Waggler' float with hemp/caster as loose feed. First, the float: it derives its name from the fact that it is locked on the line between two shots an inch apart, permitting it to waggle. The length of the float is governed mainly by conditions, the stronger the wind and/or speed of current the longer, most times, it should be. The float is attached by the bottom only, the line sunk or partially so. In a downstream wind (in an upstream wind it does not usually matter) the longer the float is and the more line sunk close to it, the less likely it is that presentation will be affected.

As with most things piscatorial, the Waggler aroused controversy. As I have said it is fished bottom only with shots placed either side of it an inch apart, and it was these locking shots which caused a flood of letters to the angling press with Dick Walker in the centre of it all. Dick questioned the necessity of the locking shots and said why not have the weight inside the float—or why use them anyway? Dick spoke strongly of inertia and on that point he is right. I hate to disagree with Dick but having those locking shots where they are, not only makes distance casting easier but, equally important, more accurate too. Having used a 'Waggler' alongside other floats I know which float I would rather use for this type of fishing. On the 'Waggler' controversy I'll say no more.

SHOTTING PATTERN FOR WAGGLER

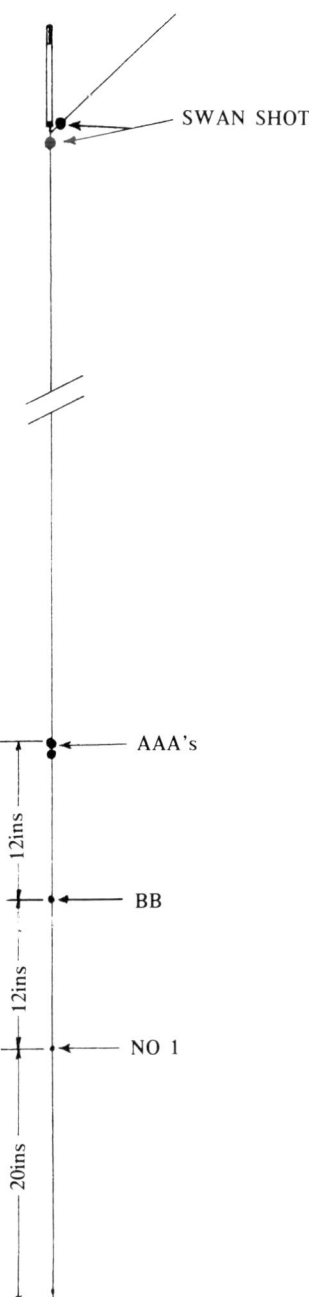

FIG 7

Due to the very fine tackle, initially I said (foolishly, as events were to prove) that the chances of landing chub in excess of four pounds, especially when close to snags, were minimal. For no matter how successful a method is, if it results in fish swimming around trailing yards of nylon—a hook length even—I want nothing to do with it. Not that I never get broken on fish—far from it—but when I do it is rarely because of my tackle and never because that tackle gives the fish more than an outside chance.

The technique had been introduced by matchmen for whom I have the greatest respect but despite its obvious success I decided to have nothing to do with it. Sometime later, however, John Everard tried it. Not only did John catch a lot of chub, he caught big ones too —and equally important—reported very few tackle breakages. John, a big-fish man of the highest order, took to the method like a duck to water and some of his catches were incredible. I just *had* to give it a try.

Now, shotting: the first essential is that at all times the shot nearest the hook should drag bottom, the float dragging the shot along. Because of this there should be at least an inch of the float standing proud of the surface; if not, when the line is checked or the dragging shot drags more than it should, the float will go under. It is best though not to check or mend the line more than is necessary but to allow the float to do it for you.

Many 'Waggler' experts pay out line as the float travels downriver, thus placing a bow in the line; some follow the float through, some mend what line remains on the surface. With a 'normal' float a downstream bow in the line is strictly taboo, but with a 'Waggler' it does not matter—indeed, with the bait dragging bottom it is often an advantage. Hooks should be spades or whipped to nylon.

A very important factor in Waggler fishing—some reckon *the* most important—is loose feeding, for having got the fish interested they must be kept interested. To attempt to describe the amount and the time between each introduction of feed in every possible situation would take up far too much space—in fact it would become confusing. What I shall say on this question is therefore a basis to work on in the many different situations which will eventually confront you.

Having tackled up, three or four pouchfuls of hemp/caster/ bronze maggot (of which I'll have more to say later) should be introduced at the head of the swim far enough upstream so that when it sinks (or some of it does) to the bottom it will be in front of you. The first cast is then made, and from then on a pouchful immediately prior to every trot down. Regularity is the keyword: far better a little on a regular basis than a lot periodically. As I have said, the question of feeding is a vitally important one, where timing and accuracy are essential.

Now bites: because the float is pulling the shots along, all kinds of movement will occur as the float travels downstream. When the bottom shot *really* drags it will pull the float under or almost so — hence the one inch standing proud; any less and the float will be under the surface more than above, and while the whole object of the exercise is for the float to go under you don't want it to when a fish is not responsible.

The bites you can generally expect are these: the float will disappear slowly (as if the dragging shot has pulled it under); it may travel downstream slower, or faster, than it should; it may lift slightly, or just disappear — fast! When it pulls under slightly I tighten whether I think a fish is responsible or not. At all times any suspicious movement should be investigated.

In water more than, say, 6ft in depth the bulk of the shots should be nearer the bottom than towards the float. The locking shots — 'swans' or AAA's — are placed against the float, the remainder of the shots decreasing in size from the float to the hook. Because the tackle is fine you don't strike but *pull* into a fish: that way you won't leave the fish trailing your hook and nylon around.

The effect the constant introduction of hemp/caster can have is often devastating. One day I was fishing the Thames on a cold winter day in a swim 14ft deep and gin clear. Half an hour after starting I caught a fair-sized chub 'on the drop' so I reduced the amount of hemp and introduced more casters (which sank slowly). I also replaced the 'Waggler' with a 'Stick' float with the shots evenly spaced. Eventually the chub were boiling on the surface, bites occurring long before the caster on the hook had reached the limit of its drop (5ft). All afternoon I caught chub, many between three and four pounds — it was like bleak snatching, but much more exciting!

At the beginning of this section I said that initially I was sceptical of being able to land big chub on such fine tackle especially when there are snags nearby, but it is surprising how much a 1½lb bottom and 20 hook can stand. Admittedly you can't hurry or bully your fish;

you take your time but because you don't exert undue pressure the fish does not tear around either. When a chub does decide to try to reach a snag you must hang on and hope: sometimes the chub will best you, yet not as often as you might think.

When the method first hit the headlines, hemp/caster were used as loose feed with one or two casters or a grain of hemp as hookbait. Later, bronze maggot became popular (during the hemp/caster period Dave Thomas had been hammering fish on the Trent with bronze maggot) and as I write the hemp/caster combination has taken a back seat. But fashions change and I have no doubt that hemp and caster will make a comeback — if they have not done so already.

Done properly, Waggler fishing is hard work. The introduction of loose feed prior to every cast; accurate casting, concentration, plus the fact you fish standing up — not to mention the time it takes to land a good fish — make it very tiring fishing indeed. That the Waggler hemp/caster/bronze maggot combination is a fine method of catching chub — and where bags are concerned the finest — there is no doubt. The one reservation I have concerns newcomers to fishing, for this is a method to be used only by anglers who know how to handle tackle correctly and to play big, and medium-sized, fish. Where inexperienced anglers are concerned, other methods, using heavier tackle, should first be accomplished.

Stick float with hemp/caster/bronze maggot/bread

Although in some situations a 'Stick' float will catch chub when others may fail, I shall not say too much about it simply because it is a method for fishing close in, and as I said earlier I don't usually find float fishing close in very effective. Nevertheless it should be mentioned.

The 'Stick' is an extremely buoyant float made with a cane stem and a carefully built-in balsa tip. The main feature of the float is that it permits very delicate presentation of baits fished on small hooks in conjunction with fine lines, and that it performs best when fished little more than a rod's length out. At all times the float is fished double-rubber. Unfortunately, the 'Stick' has one major disadvantage: that to perform properly, conditions must be absolutely right; the wind must be gentle and upstream and the surface smooth — 'boily' swims are not suited to the 'Stick'. Shotting is important and

SHOTTING FOR STICK FLOAT

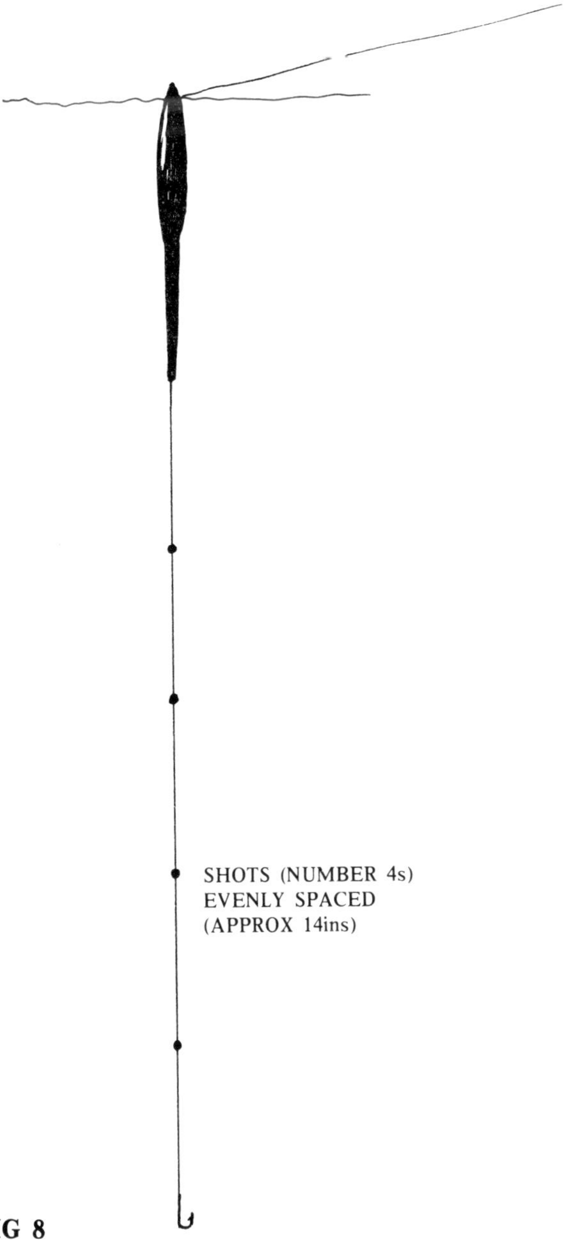

SHOTS (NUMBER 4s)
EVENLY SPACED
(APPROX 14ins)

FIG 8

although different shotting patterns are used to suit certain conditions, the basic style is to space the shots evenly starting with a 'dust' 12ins from the hook, then a number 6 and a 4, finishing with a BB. (Some anglers place this one directly under the float.)

When fishing casters, the Stick is often positioned 12ins over depth with the tackle held back slightly at intervals during its passage through the swim, making the bait lift just off bottom. At the completion of the run-through, the float is checked again, careful watch being needed at all times for a bite which may occur at any time.

When fishing caster(s) a regular introduction of loose feed is essential, the amount depending upon how fast bites/chub are coming. You don't *have* to use casters with a Stick float though; maggots and bread are also good.

I never use the Stick in wide rivers, only in narrow ones and then only rarely. Except where the water is deep with bankside cover, encouraging chub to feed under the rod top is, most times, difficult; the very act of netting a fish usually being sufficient to put the others down.

RIVERS (FREE-LINED BAITS)

Crust

The morning was hot with just a whisper of wind ruffling the surface. We, Ted Robbins and I, were fishing the Upper Thames and I eventually found myself opposite some hawthorn bushes overhanging the far bank. Past attempts to winkle a chub out by trotting bread close to the brambles had proved fruitless but big chub, I knew, lived there . . .

For once the wind was blowing from behind—ideal conditions for presenting floating crust right under the branches (where it was impossible to place a float—why I think trotted bread had proved useless). Taking a big piece of crust from a new loaf I dunked it in the water to give it extra weight and threw it against the far bank and well upstream of the brambles. Several minutes later, with the wind keeping it on course, it reached the brambles, the current swept it under and s...u...c...k—it had gone.

Seconds later a smaller piece was against the far bank, this time attached to a number 6 hook and a well-greased 3lb line. Reaching the brambles it floated under, a 'hump' appeared under the crust,

A sight not often seen: several chub taking loose pieces of crust off the surface.

then another 'hump' and it was gone. Tightening, then (as when trotting) taking several steps backwards, I got it away from the brambles and into open water: 4lb 9oz.

I am often asked what is the best method for catching better-than-average chub: the answer is floating crust. Just why floating crust should sort out the bigger chub I find difficult to understand. You can trot bread through a swim and catch four chub around two or three pounds, then put a piece of floating crust out, and bingo — a 'four'. I've done that more times than I can remember. Another thing: it is such a consistent method too. I've caught chub on floating crust on days so hot any self-respecting chub should be taking an afternoon nap; in flood water, against rafts of rubbish, in flooded meadows and once over an ice-hole. Having said that, let me make one thing clear: catching chub on floating crust consistently is not easy. But done correctly — and there is more to it than simply floating a piece of bread downriver — it is a deadly method indeed.

Usually I use a 3lb line; while a 4lb line will not, most days, deter a chub, a 5lb line definitely does. And it *must* float; that is very important. Hooks are 6's and 8's.

Now the crust itself. Crusty bread is strictly taboo, likewise bread more than two days old. The loaves I use have nice square sides and the crust is soft. Never must the bread be over-baked and if it is of any help I buy mine from the Co-op! Where casts of more than, say, 15 yards are necessary the corners of the loaf are best. Take a piece from the flat sides and you will find your range limited and accurate casting impossible. So, unless you are fishing close in, use a corner piece. Push the hook through from the crust side, out of the crumb then back into the crust. Immediately before you cast momentarily 'dunk' the crust in the water to give it extra weight.

Prior to casting — usually while tackling up — I either throw or catapult two or three pieces of crust into the water. These sample pieces are big, about 3ins square (big pieces of crumb, providing you don't squeeze them too hard, are just as good). Immediately a piece is attacked or taken — and on the right day it invariably will be — you're in business! Although the big piece(s) may have been taken without much ado, *don't* put a similar-sized piece on the hook. In my early days I missed a lot of takes and wondered why. One day however I was fishing the Avon at Bickton and the sun was beating down into the gin-clear water. Against the far bank two sample pieces were taken, followed by another big piece with my hook inside. Nothing! After three misses I stood on a higher piece of ground and watched. A chub rose to the crust, took it in then swam off *with the crust still between its lips*. Daft-like I struck, the crust came off, the chub turned and for the second time, took it again — this time for keeps . . .

Since then my bite/hooking ratio has increased enormously. Smaller pieces I discovered were not submerged and played with but swallowed immediately. Equally important, I stopped striking (or rather tightening) immediately the crust disappeared, tightening *only* when the line started moving, *not before*. Even with small pieces of crust takes will be missed; but wait for the line to move and most times you're 'in'. Inexperienced anglers usually expect the crust to disappear in a swirl but this is not always so. Some takes, especially when wind is ruffling the surface, are often minute, difficult to see, and if you are not watching *very* closely often pass unnoticed. The first time I took Fred Towns chubbing with floating crust we were watching Fred's piece of crust floating down-river some ten yards from the bank when suddenly it was not there any more. Admittedly the surface was ruffled; even so I had never before 'seen' crust disappear without actually seeing it, and told Fred to tighten. On the end was a 4lb plus chub!

On another occasion—on a calm surface this time—my crust suddenly was not there, yet—and although this may sound strange—I had not taken my eyes off it. Not even a tiny ripple was visible so I tightened: nothing. Pondering on what had happened I went to re-bait only to find the hook wasn't there. Not only had I missed seeing the take—which must have been very gentle indeed—the chub had swallowed both crust and hook and bitten the hook off. Never before, nor since, have I experienced anything like that.

At one time I considered floating crust a method effective only during summer and autumn, but I was wrong. The penny dropped one winter's day during flood conditions when I broke up what remained of a loaf and threw it into the water, and a piece of it lodged against a pile of rubbish. Shortly after I was surprised to see it disappear and when a few weeks later I watched a repeat performance immediately following a snowstorm I was not slow in placing another piece against the raft—this time with a hook inside. That afternoon four good chub, including a 'four', went back a lot wiser . . .

Since then I have taken plenty of chub on crust in winter, once as I said earlier over an ice-hole and once among long grass in a flooded field. Although the majority of chub I have caught on crust have taken it when lodged against something, or floating down close to cover, I have caught them in 'open' water also. From experience if I were asked to name the most favourable conditions for floating crust in winter I would say high, coloured water with an obstruction of some sort for the crust to rest against. The method is not, however, as effective as in summer and autumn when, on the right day—or part of a day—chub often suddenly 'come on' to crust then suddenly go off again, which I find strange. Nevertheless in winter, fished in the right place at the right time, floating crust will sometimes save what otherwise would be a blank day.

Free-lined flake

It was a warm September evening and I was fishing the Kennet. In several feet of clear water immediately upstream of an overhanging willow, a shoal of good-sized roach and a few chub periodically ventured out from the branches, intercepting passing food before disappearing again, a situation I knew where free-lined flake would teach those chub a lesson. On a 3lb line I tied a number 8 hook on which I placed a piece of flake. Making a trial cast well upstream of the branches I watched closely the behaviour of the flake, which after travelling several feet was still only inches below the surface—not deep enough as the fish were about 3ft down. Twenty inches above the hook I placed an AAA shot and tried again. The flake, as it was taken along by the current, sank deeper and deeper and when it had reached the branches was at just the right depth. Out came a chub, the lips opened, the flake disappeared and my eyes shot to the line which immediately gave a twitch—and that was one chub less to worry about.

Free-lined flake—well, that's not always true—the split shots, remember?—has brought me dozens of chub in situations ranging from turbulent water to streams little more than a few feet across where current was negligible but where there was cover both in the water and/or on the bank.

In weirpools, fast-flowing streams, or deep, slow-moving rivers, bread mashed to a pulp introduced prior to fishing and sometimes during the session on the little and often principle, will activate chub and keep them interested despite the occasional disappearance of their companions. In the right conditions—like those already mentioned but when only a shortish cast is necessary—free-lined flake is often better than floating crust. Unlike crust, however, the size of the flake is not critical mainly I think because the line close to the flake is sunk and does not therefore arouse suspicion. Because flake lacks weight, casting is difficult at distances of more than, say, 15 yards although 'dunking' it in the water helps.

In describing the session on the Kennet I mentioned pinching an AAA shot on the line just above the bait—a tactic often necessary both in fast and not so fast waters; sometimes when distance is necessary too. The secret of this, and it is an important one, is to make sure the amount of shot does not result in the flake sinking too quickly and thus behaving in an unnatural manner. At all times the weight of the flake must counteract that of the shot(s) so that, despite the addition of weight, the flake still sinks slowly and naturally. Where the flake and 'take' cannot be seen, bites are determined by watching the line where it enters the water, the strike being made when any suspicious movement occurs. Although primarily a method for the warmer weather, free-lined flake is effective during mild spells in winter too when the chub are active.

SMALL RIVERS

Close to my home is a small tributary of the Thames no more than ten yards wide and shallow (4-5ft). Although a chub weighing 5lb 7oz was once taken, on average they ran to around 3½lbs. For many years I fished the stream from which I learnt a great deal. In one swim the branches of a fallen willow touched the surface over four feet of water. Chub were always present and it was a bad session indeed if at least three did not oblige—often in as many casts. My set-up was simple: 4lb line with one, sometimes two, swan shots pinched on the line, 15in from the hook for cheesepaste, 4in for crust. Getting the weight right was important for the lead had to roll but *only just*.

Casting underarm some five yards upstream of the branches I placed the bait opposite where I was crouching then, immediately it hit bottom, paid out 4ft of line. This put a bow in it which because I was fishing on a short line was important. With the line between two fingers I pointed the rod at the bait following the line as the current moved it round, the lead *just* rolling bottom. Bites were determined by feel alone with most times just one 'knock' being felt—nothing else. By striking immediately the knock was felt it was impossible to miss—it was that easy. But I did not just hold the line; I watched it too at the point where it entered the water. Sometimes the line would move slowly, so much so the movement was difficult to see—and not downstream but up. I didn't miss those either!

At another point along the stream a wire fence 4ft above the bank made fishing difficult, but chub were always present and most times one—only one (why you will see in a minute)—would end up in my net. On the 4lb line I attached a float double-rubber. The float, no more than 4in in length had a shot loading of about one swan shot but because the float was set 6ins over depth the shot loading was not important. With crust or cheesepaste on a number 8 hook and standing well back from the water (so I could just see the float) I lowered float and bait into the water then, as the shot touched bottom, held the line clear of the water so the float was lying at half-cock. When a chub picked up the bait—which usually occurred within a minute—the float, still at half-cock, would slowly move towards midstream. Rarely did I miss a bite but because the landing net had to be placed right in the swim most times it was the only one.

When legering, a bite often occurs either immediately the lead moves or, when fishing hard on the bottom, you move the lead by pulling on the line. Many anglers believe the bait suddenly moves downstream and when rolling the bottom this, most times, is true; but when fishing hard on the bottom and you pull the line the bait moves *upstream*.

One day I was fishing the little stream when it was bitterly cold and the water gin clear. Against the far bank, in less than 3ft of water, I spotted a fair-sized chub lying completely still. Crawling into position just downstream of the chub I cast a piece of cheesepaste 3ft in front of it. To my surprise I had too much weight on and instead of the bait trundling down towards the chub it remained still. Two minutes later the chub decided to investigate and slowly approached the bait. When some 6ins away the chub stopped; a minute passed, the chub was still there, and thinking it might take the bait if it moved I pulled on the line. As I did so the bait moved *upstream* and a minute later that chub was regretting its folly.

I am not suggesting a bait *always* moves upstream when the line is pulled: depth of water and angle of the line are just two factors which may decide otherwise. But because that chub took my bait when behaving in such an unnatural manner it encouraged me when fishing a stationary bait to pull the line more than I had previously, a technique which over the years has put a lot of chub on the bank.

In the Introduction I said chub eat almost anything. At one time before their numbers decreased rapidly, frogs accounted for many chub but no-one, least of all me, would in these conservation-minded days recommend their use. At one time I caught chub on whole freshwater mussel, but I have not used one for years and don't consider them worthy of discussion although on hard-fished waters — and where mussels are prolific — they make a useful 'change' bait. Mussels are fished whole, the hook — a number 6 or 4 — pushed once through the orange part.

Other fine baits are worms, slugs and crayfish, which do warrant discussion. All species of fish take worms and chub are no exception. In high, coloured water a worm fished on a conventional leger rig will often tempt chub when other baits fail and the bigger the worm is,

---

'Chub-chasing'. Seconds after this photo was taken the author extracted a four-pounder from this not-easy-to-fish spot.

most times, the better. Many anglers pass the hook through a worm two or three times thereby tying it in a knot. I've always believed however that a bait should be presented as a fish expects to find it and I'm sure chub don't expect to find a worm tied in a knot! At all times I like a worm to behave naturally and to achieve this I pass the hook through once, half an inch from the top of its head. The fact that the hook shows matters not one iota, although I do prefer a bronze-coloured hook to a gold one. Having said that, I don't think the colour of the hook is very important.

When fishing small streams and rivers I prefer to present my worm on a weightless, floatless line especially when stalking chub. In such situations difficulty may be experienced casting a single lob any distance, particularly if using, say, a 6lb line—which is often necessary where chub are lying in heavily-overgrown swims. The answer, however, is not to increase casting weight by adding lead but to take Fred J. Taylor's advice and use two worms! At most times I freeline lobs on a 3lb line but when there is danger of losing fish in snags I step this up to 6lb, sometimes heavier.

In the 60's when I fished the Ouse above Buckingham the river was full of bulrushes and in many swims it was necessary to hold the chub immediately the hook went home. One day I spotted a huge chub behind a patch of rushes and after weighing up the situation decided to use a 9lb line. As the crayfish hit the water the chub took it in and I held on, but not for long because seconds later the line broke . . .

On another occasion in similar circumstances Dick Walker was smashed on an 11lb line. Many will say you should not get broken on 9 and 11lb line and most times you shouldn't, but these were very 'hairy' situations indeed—and the chub *big*.

Slugs—those big, black, slimy characters found in wet grass are a favourite chub dish which, like worms, are free-lined, the hook (number 6 or 4) passed through the slug once. Being heavy they cast well and for the majority of situations no lead is necessary.

Like frogs, the crayfish population has, due to pollution and abstraction, declined rapidly over the years but where they still exist in numbers they remain a fine bait.

One day I was fishing the Ouse at Buckingham in company with Dick Walker and the Taylor brothers, our guests being two young lads who had won a prize (a day with us) in a competition. My 'brief' was to catch a big chub (I eventually nobbled a four and a quarter pounder with one lad watching) but before that I fluffed an opportunity which I could not expect again that day—and which in the event didn't occur. This taught me a lesson: *never* allow your concentration to be distracted. Having attached a crayfish to a number 4 hook I crept into position and cast to where I thought a big chub might be. After allowing it to sink to the bottom I retrieved it in small jerks (to imitate its natural movement—it was hooked in the tail) but there was no response and when it was some 12ft from the bank I foolishly turned round to speak to Fred, who was watching. As I did so a cry of 'watch it' from Fred made me look back just in time to see a very big chub immediately behind the cray and obviously intent on taking it. But the movement of turning back round proved my undoing, the chub spotted me and bolted. That was an awful mistake on my part: always keep your mind on what you are doing until the bait is out of the water.

The manner in which a cray is hooked is important. After killing it, pass the hook through the second segment from the tail from *underneath* so the point protrudes from the top. If you pass the hook through the opposite way the point will be masked by the cray's tail with the chance of hooking the chub virtually impossible.

78 FISHING FOR BIG CHUB

A four-pounder among miniature ice-bergs.

6 Ice Holes

In 1963 the country suffered one of its most severe winters. For six weeks rivers and stillwaters were frozen often to a depth of 2ft and more, and for most anglers fishing was non-existent. But I was one of the lucky ones. With so many waters of varying character close to home I was able to fish somewhere and in the event missed only one weekend's fishing.

Wherever I fished it meant breaking the ice but having fished in ice-holes before such experiences were not new. The first job was to find a swim where I knew the water was at least 4ft deep and where the ice was thin enough to force a hole. The next job was to find something to make a 3ft hole with (usually a big branch); that being accomplished I then sprinkled a few maggots into the hole and tackled up.

I arrived one morning and after these preliminaries tackled up with a 3lb line, a float carrying one BB shot which sank it to within half an inch of the surface and a 16 hook; bait, one maggot.

By this time a thin layer of ice had formed over the hole which I scooped out with the landing net, introduced a few more maggots and lowered my tackle into the hole. Almost immediately I noticed a tiny 'ring' around the float—nothing more. I struck, expecting a small fish, but a heavy fish bored down under the ice and I was forced to give line. Quickly I thrust the rod top under water to prevent the ice cutting the line and gently played the fish in that position. Eventually a three pound chub surfaced: I pulled its head on to the ice, the rest quickly followed and I slid it over to the bank. Another small hole was broken against the bank to house the keepnet, more maggots were thrown into the hole, I rebaited and cast.

This time I had to wait a little longer by which time ice was forming round the float. This I broke by tapping it gently with the rod

Netting a chub from an ice-hole.

top. The ripple had barely died away when another tiny 'ring' appeared round the float. A second later I was playing another good chub again with the rod top under the water. Three and a half pounds.

An hour later I decided to move. There were now five chub in the net but I hadn't had a bite for some time, and breaking another hole further along I adopted the same procedure as before. Once again I caught a chub immediately I started fishing, quickly followed by three more. The chub were taking the single maggot almost as soon as the float had settled, but due to the intense cold I was missing bites. I didn't like the thought of packing up with the fish going so well, yet I knew I could not take much more. Just time, I thought, to have another cast in my original swim. Again the branch came into play and the job of removing the ice was gone through again. Two more chub were the result then, with the icy air almost unbearable, I called it a day.

Although 1963 was exceptionally severe (one day with dozens of others, some on pushbikes, I walked three miles into Oxford over the middle of the Thames), '63 was not the last time I caught chub in ice

Should the landing net be frozen the chub is slid over the ice!

holes. Most times the methods and tackle I have described have sufficed, although it is better I think if the float is shotted so that only ¼″ stands out of the water. Some days the hook must be smaller too — 18's and 20's.

    What must always be remembered is that immediately a chub is hooked, thrust the rod top under the water and play the chub with the rod in that position. Failure to do so will invariably result in the ice cutting the line. When the fish is ready for netting the rod top is brought above the surface again with two options open: either the chub is netted or, if that proves difficult (usually because the net is frozen solid!), pulled out of the hole and slid over the ice. It is important too to make sure the hole is no further out than the length of your rod.

    On days when the air temperature is below freezing ice will keep forming over the hole. In really severe weather it will be necessary to clear the hole every two minutes or so, yet this does not frighten the chub. Even more remarkable is that the act of smashing a hole does

A chub is pulled unceremoniously across thick ice after being hooked against the far bank in the only piece of ice-free water.

not either, the first bite often coming within minutes of fishing. Fish, I firmly believe, are attracted to the sudden influx of light — if you want to learn more ask the Eskimos!

Ice-hole fishing is not something I wish to do very often and where our winters are concerned the opportunities are limited anyway. Nevertheless, it is a fascinating technique and as I have proved several times, a deadly one too; and *very* exciting.

7 Stillwaters

Legering

The first time I legered for chub in a stillwater was in 1968. Having heard reports of chub being caught in a gravel pit I obtained a ticket and arrived one evening in March just before it got dark. Knowing nothing about the water I chose a swim where the plummet revealed a clean bottom and decided to leger cheesepaste with two swan shots pinched on the line. I had no indicators and the bites (of which I had eight) were detected by a small piece of paste pinched on the line between reel and butt ring. That night I caught my first-ever stillwater chub on a leger (I caught six) on a set-up which was simple to say the least!

From then on I caught more chub from that and other pits on bread, cheesepaste, and luncheon meat. There was nothing fancy about my set-ups; crust and flake I fished with the lead as light as possible stopped some 6ins away; for cheesepaste about 16ins away. Bites, at most times, were definite, the bobbin (by then I was using cork models) lifting, dropping, sometimes a lot, sometimes hardly at all, but all confident bites. Although fishing was not easy with blank days (and nights) common, I learnt a lot and in the process put a lot of big chub on the bank.

In January 1972 Geoff Barnes and I decided to concentrate on the pit where my baptism with stillwater chub had taken place four years previously. We fished both day and night, with best results coming after dark with most of the chub—including many four-pounders falling to luncheon meat. This initially—for me that is—caused problems. Geoff and I fished two swims some 20 yards apart and it slowly—too slowly—dawned on me that I missed far more bites than Geoff, a matter which one night was brought to a head.

As I said, we fished luncheon meat (incidentally the brand the chub appeared to like best was Wall's Bacon Slice), my set-up being

¾in cubes on a number 8 hook, tied direct to 6lb line, the lead stopped some 15ins from the hook. Bites varied, sometimes the bobbin hanging 15ins below the rod would smack the butt before you could say 'chub' (these were very difficult to hook—and at night, when all you saw was the Beta-lite whizzing skywards, quite alarming too!); sometimes it dropped back slowly (those were invariably missed; if it dropped back fast you invariably hooked them and sometimes it travelled towards the rod in small jerks, bites which were unmissable).

One night I missed seventeen bites during which time Geoff didn't have one. Then I hooked one—4¾lbs. On the next cast I hooked another; at the same time Geoff hooked one too. Both fish were landed, mine weighed 5lb 1oz, Geoff's 5lb 7oz. Shortly after, Geoff nobbled another of 4lb 3oz—his only two bites that evening.

I went home worried about those missed bites, for obviously something was wrong. The next time we went I watched Geoff cut his luncheon meat and noticed he used much smaller pieces than I did; also, his length of tail was much longer—about 24ins. Smaller pieces of meat, a longer tail: was that, I wondered, the answer?

Apparently so, because immediately my bite/hooking ratio increased dramatically. The bottom of the pit was very clean and heavily fished—and chub learn. Without doubt they were picking up my meat, swimming off with it lightly between their lips but feeling the lead which deterred them from swallowing it. With my short tail the lead was being felt almost as soon as the bait was picked up, but Geoff's longer one permitted them to take much more line before they pulled on the lead proper. Rarely does the tail land in a straight line; consequently the chub felt very little, if anything, by the time the lead was moved by which time they had swallowed the bait. Whether the bait size made any difference is difficult to say, but the length of tail, I am convinced, did.

The question of the amount of loose feed you wish to introduce prior to and during fishing should be considered very carefully: some days a lot will be necessary, on others very little. As a general rule I catapult about six cubes into an area of, say, five square yards where I intend casting then wait and see what happens. When a bite occurs —whether I hook the fish or not—I introduce four or five more pieces.

These came in successive casts—5lb 1oz, 4¾lb. ▶

Should bites continue at fairly frequent intervals — say every quarter of an hour — two or three more pieces are introduced as each bite occurs. With chub present and obviously feeding, such introductions will keep them interested yet at the same time are not sufficient to stuff their bellies full — although some days it appears impossible to do that. Immediately bites cease or slow down considerably, no further introductions are made.

In pits with clean bottoms — clean enough that is for chub to pick up a bait without difficulty — maggots and casters fished in conjunction with a feeder are often successful.

Having selected a swim — and in daytime the further it is from the bank the better — I attach a Drennan Feederlink to the line, stopped some 20ins from the hook. The manner in which the feeder is attached depends mainly upon the whim of the angler; some like it fixed, others sliding. I prefer the latter.

My first job is to replace the ring on the link running through the feeder with a swivel (for this another length of nylon will be required) then, having passed the main line through the swivel I tie another swivel on the end of the line. The hook — 14 for maggots, 16 for caster — is attached to another length of nylon some 20ins in length which in turn is attached to the swivel. Although this set-up entails two knots it is, I find, better than a leger stop which as the feeder hits it sometimes slips on the strike.

Usually I fish three maggots, the size of the feeder depending upon the number of maggots you wish to introduce. Most times I use the middle size which holds 30-40 maggots. Once cast, the bait is left for I don't like retrieving unless (a), a bite occurs (obviously) or (b), when it has been in the water a long time (and the maggots have dispersed). Casters I use only occasionally simply because they demand a fine hook length and most of the stillwaters I fish are weedy.

Where considered necessary however, one or two on a 16 or 18 hook on 1-1½lb bottoms is all right but the feeder needs to be the open-end type with cereal at either end to retain the casters during casting. The consistency of the cereal is important; too hard and it won't disperse or will take a long time to do so; too wet and it will fall out.

This photograph clearly shows the immaculate condition of the author's seven-pounder.

Bites vary with 'twitchers' commonplace, for a chub when it finds them does not have to move far, if at all, to mop them up — hence the minute bites. This occurrence — a common one in tench fishing (see Gravel Pit Angling) — often results in the bobbin moving less than an inch where the slightest delay will result either in the maggots being sucked, the casters shelled, or the hook being bitten off by the throat teeth. Hitting twitch bites consistently is not easy: at all times great concentration is required, with your striking hand close to the rod and the bobbin sheltered from the wind enabling these minute, yet confident, bites to be detected.

Float fishing

In 1974 John Everard decided to fish a pit he had never fished before and in one afternoon caught three chub weighing 3lb 14oz, 4lb 8oz and 4lb 12oz, and followed those up the following season with one 5lb 6oz, all taken on maggots on a number 14 hook attached to 3lb line under a 'Windbeater' float, close in. I'm telling this because John's tactics would appear very successful and on those two days they were. But only then, for subsequent trips using identical tactics failed to put another chub on the bank.

Over the years I have tried similar tactics in other pits but, night excepted, results have been poor. In saying this I am not suggesting this applies to *all* stillwaters, only those I have experience of, but because they have proved successful at night (when the chub come in close) they are worth relating.

My set-up is simple: 3lb line, 'Windbeater' float with a shot loading of around two swan shots, 14 or 16 hook. Most of the chub I have taken on this set-up have picked the bait up off the bottom, bites consisting of lifts, dips, and slow sink-aways — bites you would expect from other species, like, say, roach. Deep water close in, especially with snags and ledges nearby, are the places I seek with, of course, quietness and concealment essential at all times.

Regarding loose feeding, at night I usually introduce a pouchful, say, every half an hour but in waters where the chub population is high or appears to be so, and where bites come at regular intervals, the amount can be increased. The type of water is important and in those where bites are expected to be few and far between the amount of loose feed should be considered carefully, although a lot is often eaten by just one chub entering the swim. In these situations however

I believe crust or flake are better with a little cereal around the bait—sometimes none at all. Like tench, chub in pits are cruisers and where they grow large, crust and flake are good which—important this—in clear water can be seen a considerable distance away by cruising fish.

One day Geoff was fishing crust on a link leger some 12ft over the margin when a chub appeared several feet away from his bait, swimming towards him (unusual behaviour in daylight). Suddenly, although the crust was on the chub's off side, it changed course, and swam towards the crust, at the same time going deeper. Seconds later Geoff's bobbin lifted and a 5lb 8oz chub had learnt a lesson.

That incident demonstrated quite clearly the distance chub can see a big bait; when Geoff first saw the chub it was only just under the surface yet Geoff's crust was several feet to one side of it on the bottom in 8ft of water.

In one pit the chub average 2-2½lbs and on several occasions, just for a bit of fun, I have fished for them with casters under a float. Sometimes the chub prefer the caster(s) falling through the water where a float with a thin antenna and a 2lb line with a number 18 hook attached to 1lb bottom proves deadly. The shots are spread, with the bottom shot (a dust) 20ins from the bait. Bites, most days, are definite and easy to hook. Some days however the chub prefer the bait hard on the bottom. Here, a 'Windbeater' is better but bites are difficult to detect, often resulting in only half the sight bob disappearing with an immediate response essential. For both methods I introduce a pouchful of casters every ten minutes or so, a little longer if bites are a long time coming. On such days I don't think the chub are interested in quantities of feed. This is enjoyable fishing and it is successful in daytime too, but it requires a matchman's approach to derive full benefit. I don't employ the method often, only when I want a bit of fun fishing.

At the beginning of this chapter I mentioned a small pit where I caught my first-ever stillwater chub on a leger. The following year we discovered the water also held large roach to which Fred Towns, John Everard and I turned our attention. We fished with maggots under 'Windbeater' floats, our best catches coming after dark with our floats illuminated by cycle lamps (Beta-lites were unheard of then)—which brings me to the chub.

During two memorable years spent roach fishing we caught many chub, a considerable number over four pounds. Most of the 'fours' were taken on number 18 hooks, 1½lb bottoms and single

maggot fished close in, under, as I have said, an illuminated float. At that time everything I had read regarding lights said it was vital the light did not penetrate the water and that the torch beam just skimmed the surface. That was how we fished, but one night an incident occurred which forced me to change my views.

John Everard and I were fishing together; the bank was low and John's front rod rest was positioned in 18ins of water some two feet from the bank. His cycle lamp was at ground level two feet behind the rest. The bottom of the pit just past John's front rest was bathed in light before the beam picked out the float some 15ft away. Suddenly a big roach appeared and began mopping up loose maggots around the rod rest. That a roach—and a big roach too—should be so brave as to come and feed only two feet from a powerful light astonished us both and I decided to try and catch it. Changing to a smaller and lighter float I cast against John's front rest, the float dipped and I was 'in', but it wasn't a roach that had picked up my maggot but a *chub*.

Now then, that night two fish, a chub and a roach, had ventured into a light shining *right into the water* and I wondered: were fish as scared of lights as we believed? In rivers I have watched barbel on the bottom in torchlight; it was interesting . . .

A few nights later I fished the pit again with Fred Towns. Fred had difficulty getting his lamp to remain in position and finally decided to carry on fishing with the beam shining directly into the water around his float. That night Fred caught roach and chub and it was obvious that a torch beam penetrating the surface did not frighten the fish one iota.

These days I never worry if the beam from my torch shines directly into the water for I am convinced it makes little difference. What I don't do is keep moving the torch; once in position it remains there, each cast being made into the beam *not*, as I have seen anglers doing, casting then picking the float out with the torch. Whether a moving light frightens fish I don't know—I think it probably does— but when I'm not sure about anything I don't practise it. Remember too I only use cycle lamps—not Tilleys which I think *do* scare fish— and make if uncomfortable for nearby anglers too.

Four four-pounders taken from a stillwater by Peter Drennan and the author:
4lb 14oz, 4lb 10oz, 4lb 8oz, 4lb 2oz.

Today, Beta-lites mean I use torches far less. In some circumstances however — when for instance gazing for several hours at a Beta-lite causes eye strain (eventually I am seeing two Beta-lites), I prefer to illuminate my float with a torch.

Deadbaits

When I was at school hardly a week passed when my family did not dine on eel caught by my father on night lines. Sometimes I was allowed to help set the lines which was a great thrill and sometimes (if they had been set on a Friday evening) allowed to help pick them up the following morning — an even greater thrill. Father's night lines consisted of balls of string with several 'droppers' also of string, some 19ins in length with a large 'eel hook' attached to each dropper. Bait was either gudgeon or bleak threaded. With sufficient lead to hold bottom, the line was thrown into the river then attached to either a large stone or bankside rushes.

The following morning we would arrive at daybreak to find at least one eel attached to each line. But eels were not all we caught; chub — big chub too — were often attached, and one morning we had four on one line. Thankfully, unlike the eels, the chub were still alive and returned. (In those days immediately prior to and during the War when food was short, setting night lines in my neck of the woods was common practice, but the setting of fixed night lines is illegal.)

Obviously it did not take me long to realise chub liked dead fish so I started fishing with gudgeon and bleak on what was then my standard barbel gear — number 6 hook, a medicine bottle cork for a float, with the bait hooked through the top lip. Over the years I caught dozens of chub on livebaits but missed many more. Bites, most times, consisted of the float going straight under, the strike resulting in the fish being missed with only the head of the livebait remaining.

The chub, I assumed, had grabbed the bait and swallowed it tail first then, as I struck, closed its mouth, its powerful throat teeth severing the bait. Much later my bite/hooking ratio improved somewhat after I threaded the bait (dead). But more of that and the balls of string later . . .

During the late '70's news reached me of pike anglers having very fast runs on mackerel and herring in a local pit. Despite the fast runs all the bites were missed and I was asked for my views. The fish responsible I said were chub and shortly afterwards two, one of six pounds, were caught. In the autumn of '80 an 18-year-old angler, Kevin Pimm, caught a huge chub from the pit weighing 7lb 1oz. Kevin's great fish had taken half a mackerel at night intended for pike.

Four months later I received a phone call asking me to go to the pit and photograph a 'record chub'. The captor was—Kevin! Unfortunately his chub was not a record but two ounces short. That too had taken half a mackerel.

Before his first 'seven' Kevin had had several fast runs on mackerel all of which he missed. The baits were unmarked and both his 'sevens' were the result of fast runs. The runs he had missed I said were probably chub which had not swallowed the bait because of the wire trace. Greedy blighters chub may be, but they are not fools, being suspicious of anything which does not *feel* right. Past experiences had shown chub did not like baits attached to wire.

One night Kevin retreated to his tent for some shut-eye but before doing so wound in his line and to keep his mackerel away from the attention of rats dropped it into 12ins of water under his rod top. In the morning some forty yards of line had been removed and the bait gone. That was most interesting and I will return to it later.

Before I left I asked Kevin whether he was fishing the next day. He wasn't and I went home determined to put one of those big chub on the bank—but without wire. I arrived at the pit the next morning at 10 a.m. with some sprats, my 'Ultra-lite' rod and 6lb line. My intention was to free-line a sprat threaded, with a number 6 single straight to the line with a bobbin as indicator. Once in position I would remain close to the rod and—important this—should the bobbin move, strike *immediately*, for I reasoned should a chub pick up the sprat it would swallow it on the spot and by delaying the strike I would be running the risk of the chub biting through the line with its throat teeth.

When I went to my hook box however I discovered I had left my big singles at home. A rummage through the box produced some number 6 trebles which I don't like, but it was Hobson's choice so, with a baiting needle, I threaded a sprat placing one hook of the treble in the eye socket. The baiting needle was pushed through the sprat *just* under the skin so that on the strike (should one result) the line would pull out easily (see Fig 9).

MOUNTING DEADBAIT

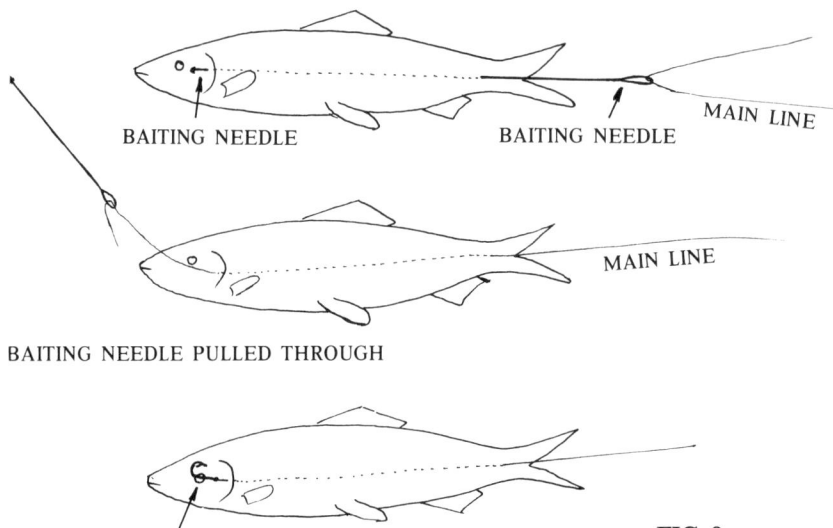

FIG 9

Eight hours later (in darkness) the bobbin rose 12ins. Way out a fish was thumping and I prayed it wasn't a pike. My prayers were answered and two minutes later I was gazing down at my best-ever chub — a magnificent fish weighing 6lb 6oz.

When I went to remove the treble I discovered to my horror it was out of sight — how I was not bitten off I shall never know. The treble proved stubborn, the fish bled badly and when half an hour later Bruce Vaughan, the deputy editor of *Coarse Fishing Monthly* arrived and it was still bleeding I put it out of its misery, took it home and set it up.

So my assumptions were correct; a bait on 6lb monofilament was swallowed immediately yet despite my prompt reponse it was already down the chub's throat, which left me in no doubt that most times chub and wire traces do not mix.

The author took this 6lb 6oz chub on sprat on his first-ever trip to a gravel pit — a remarkable piece of good fortune.

The capture of that chub fired my enthusiasm; I wanted a 'seven' and for the remainder of the season fished, on average, three evenings a week. During that time just three fish picked up my bait all of which I tightened into immediately the bobbin moved. Two were pike, best 11½lbs, which although hooked inside the mouth did not bite through the 6lb mono. The third I tightened into but felt nothing. Not only had the bait gone but the hook too—bitten off; chub! In November '81 Chris Thornton from Middlesex caught a chub weighing 7lb 2oz from the pit. The following week I was called out to photograph yet another 'seven' taken by Chris's companion Noel Hutchinson, and Peter and Noel had an interesting story to tell.

A few months previously I had written an article about chub on dead baits in which I stressed the importance of using monofilament in place of wire, and the reasons—but not forgetting the problems of deep hooking. Chris and Noel had started pike fishing and following several fast (and missed) runs *on wire* decided to discard the wire and replace it with 20lb Dacron. It was on the Dacron both seven pounders had been caught.

Chris's and Noel's decision to use Dacron was interesting. Earlier I mentioned my father's night lines made from string with the hook tied direct and obviously the thick string did not deter the chub —because it was *soft*. Whatever a hook is attached to, providing it does not affect presentation, the thickness will not most times deter the fish from taking the bait, but chub do not like the *feel* of wire no matter how thin it is.

About lines in *Still Water Angling* Dick Walker said, 'I am well convinced that fish can always see your line however fine . . . it is the feel of it they don't like—its stiffness is most unnatural. Natural filamentous things in the water are soft, not stiff.' Dick caught his 44lb carp on 12lb plaited nylon.

Chris and Noel had however taken my suggestion further: instead of placing the hooks in the head of the mackerel (they used small ones) they positioned them just above the tail—which was good thinking. Although their baits were well down the chub's throat, the chub were hooked just inside the mouth.

When I returned home after photographing Noel's fish I sat down and after some thought decided to fish the swim again. One thing bothered me however: from five huge chub caught, four had fallen to mackerel; would they, I wondered, be suspicious of them;

The capture of that chub fired my enthusiasm; I wanted a 'seven' and for the remainder of the season fished, on average, three evenings a week. During that time just three fish picked up my bait all of which I tightened into immediately the bobbin moved. Two were pike, best 11½lbs, which although hooked inside the mouth did not bite through the 6lb mono. The third I tightened into but felt nothing. Not only had the bait gone but the hook too—bitten off; chub! In November '81 Chris Thornton from Middlesex caught a chub weighing 7lb 2oz from the pit. The following week I was called out to photograph yet another 'seven' taken by Chris's companion Noel Hutchinson, and Peter and Noel had an interesting story to tell.

A few months previously I had written an article about chub on dead baits in which I stressed the importance of using monofilament in place of wire, and the reasons—but not forgetting the problems of deep hooking. Chris and Noel had started pike fishing and following several fast (and missed) runs *on wire* decided to discard the wire and replace it with 20lb Dacron. It was on the Dacron both seven pounders had been caught.

Chris's and Noel's decision to use Dacron was interesting. Earlier I mentioned my father's night lines made from string with the hook tied direct and obviously the thick string did not deter the chub —because it was *soft*. Whatever a hook is attached to, providing it does not affect presentation, the thickness will not most times deter the fish from taking the bait, but chub do not like the *feel* of wire no matter how thin it is.

About lines in *Still Water Angling* Dick Walker said, 'I am well convinced that fish can always see your line however fine . . . it is the feel of it they don't like—its stiffness is most unnatural. Natural filamentous things in the water are soft, not stiff.' Dick caught his 44lb carp on 12lb plaited nylon.

Chris and Noel had however taken my suggestion further: instead of placing the hooks in the head of the mackerel (they used small ones) they positioned them just above the tail—which was good thinking. Although their baits were well down the chub's throat, the chub were hooked just inside the mouth.

When I returned home after photographing Noel's fish I sat down and after some thought decided to fish the swim again. One thing bothered me however: from five huge chub caught, four had fallen to mackerel; would they, I wondered, be suspicious of them;

INSTANT STRIKE RIG

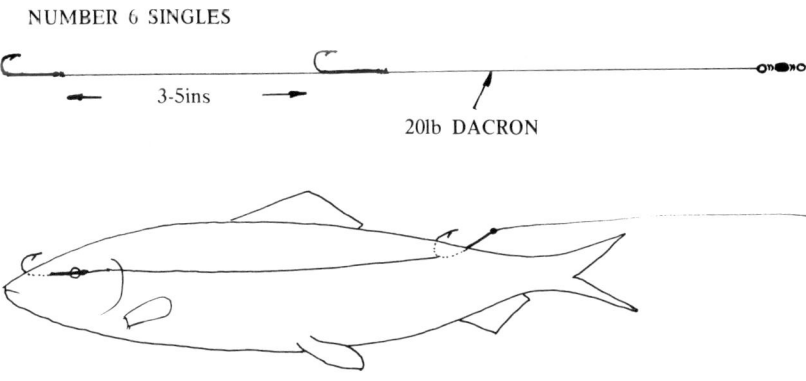

FIG 10

was in fact a 'new' bait needed. I decided it was. On my way over the following morning I called at a trout farm and picked up some 7in rainbows. On arrival I attached one to an instant-strike rig, the hooks tied on 20lb Dacron attached with a swivel to 9lb line (see Fig 10).

I cast the trout some 25 yards and was getting the line tight when I felt a 'bonk' and immediately released the line. Nothing else occurred however so I retrieved the bait to find the head almost severed but otherwise unmarked. I shall never know of course, but past experiences suggested one thing — chub. That morning I was very unlucky.

Four hours later the bobbin moved and I tightened immediately, but the fish was too heavy and several minutes later an 18lb pike was lying at my feet; a nice fish but not what I had come for.

Two days later another pike (18½lb) came my way but I was more excited when, two hours after, in darkness, the sardine was picked up. The fish did not feel too heavy, it did very little and I was excited. Ten seconds later the line went slack and with heavy heart I reeled in. The sardine from the head halfway down its flank was almost devoid of flesh. Without any doubt a chub had been responsible. In five years of using Alan Beat's instant-strike rig that was only the *second* time a fish had come off: an hour later heavy rain set in and I went home. That night the rain turned to snow, the freeze-up which was to last three weeks had begun, a period when my rods were idle.

At the first sign of the thaw my thoughts turned to the pit again and I arrived one morning at dawn to find someone already fishing. Stopping the car some fifty yards away I was deliberating what to do when an angler appeared from the shadows. It was Philip Tew from London. 'When it gets light' Philip said, 'could you photograph a big chub — it's about seven pounds'.

It weighed 7lb 1oz and had taken half a mackerel at 5 a.m., and after its picture had been taken Philip slipped it back.

Two days later I arrived at the water at 5 a.m. but had to wait three hours (just after it got light) for the bobbin to lift. Tightening immediately I was into a fish which seconds later boiled on the surface twice — a big chub. Then the line went slack; the hooks had fallen out. An hour later I was on my way home with, for the second time in a few weeks, a heavy heart . . .

That evening I returned and an hour after dark the bobbin lifted. I waited a few seconds and tightened and for the second time that day was 'in'. Seconds and several 'thumps' later however it was gone and I reeled in. Both singles were gone, the 20lb Dacron bitten through. I could have cried . . .

Then a mild spell of weather set in and that week found me at the pit six times. On the fourth night an event took place which again showed how close in chub come at night; an event which filled me with excitement and confidence that the day — or rather the night — when I would nobble a 'seven' was drawing near . . . I had decided to sit right alongside my rods and not move (previously I had sat several yards back) so, gathering my food and flask, I settled down. My front rests were in some 12ins of water and some three feet from the bank when suddenly a 'hump' appeared immediately in front of one. Seconds later another 'hump' occurred: a big fish was cruising around in 12ins of water right against the rod rest . . .

Moving very slowly I started to wind in the bait nearest me which was some 20 yards out. It had almost reached the margins when the fish apparently spotted me and bolted. I wound the sardine and left it just past the rod top in some three feet of water. An hour later the bobbin moved six inches, then stopped, and an hour later I retrieved it. The bait was unmarked, so whether it was picked up or a fish brushed into the line I shall never know. What I *do* know is that a big chub came in very close that night — not the first I had seen in shallow water against a rod rest.

My mind was then made up. On future visits I would place my baits right in the margins and sit over the rods. If other anglers were present I would have to place them further out for I was convinced a chub would not venture close in if there was bankside disturbance of any kind.

For remember: Kevin Pimm had his bait taken one night in 12ins of water under the rod top while he was asleep in the tent; I knew chub came into the margins at night in other pits and I had already proved that a bait presented on nylon (which I was not completely happy with) would be swallowed on the spot without the chub making a fast run. A bait — and by this time I was using trout and sardine exclusively — presented on Dacron, in the margins with *no one else present* — or someone keeping as quiet as me — would eventually be picked up by a huge chub. That such an event took place is now history and the events of that memorable night are told in chapter 10.

Chub chasing

In rivers, many chub are caught after the angler has stalked them — 'chub-chasing' as it is called. But chub-chasing need not be confined to rivers: stalking chub in stillwaters has brought me lots of fish especially on hot summer days when most fish are lying doggo. All that is required is a new loaf, the basic gear including a small but weighty float — Pete Drennan's 'Loaders' being ideal. On a 3lb line, tie a number 6 hook, then grease the line. Then, with just the loaf, landing net and some spare hooks and shots in your pocket, you creep around the water walking slowly and watching for signs of chub — swirls, humps or bow-waves on the surface. Having located some chub you are then faced with a choice: floating crust or flake. If the surface is ruffled, crust is a good bet, fished as described in chapter 5. In calm conditions, chub in stillwaters are often reluctant to take crust mainly I think because they can see the line, and while chub are not scared of tackle (providing it does not affect the behaviour of the bait) a line however thin on a calm surface in stillwaters does arouse the chub's suspicion.

In rivers this is not always the case, the reason I believe being that the bait is moving along and the chub has to make up its mind quickly whether to take it or not. In stillwaters it has all the time it wants to decide; even when there is competition from others present crust in calm conditions is, in my experience, most times refused.

In flat calms therefore I prefer flake either free-lined or under a float. In the former case you cannot cast very far, not that distance is always important. Two years ago I spotted a big chub less than 15ft from the bank; the water was calm, the sun beating down. A piece of crust was inspected but refused, so striking it off (better than than to pull it back and possibly scare the fish) I replaced it with a piece of flake. I watched it sink and when some 2ft down the line began to move. The chub weighed 4¾lbs and illustrated perfectly the importance of having the line sunk, when the chub are far less suspicious.

Sometimes the chub are too far out to cast free-lined flake to, and on such days the float really scores. Get a 'Loader' with a shot loading of one or two swan shot (depending on how far you have to cast), attach it double rubber and about 3ft from the bait with the shot(s) halfway between the float and bait.

Now the important bit. The cast must be such that the chub reaches the flake before it reaches the limit of its drop. A piece of bread suspended below the surface does not look right—to a fish even less so. I have already illustrated the importance of this when describing earlier a huge chub I saw on a bar: here's another.

One day I spotted several large chub cruising beneath the surface and as it was calm I decided a float would give me the best chance. Minutes later I noticed the flake suspended with several large chub milling round it—just looking. Suddenly the flake disappeared; at the same time the float tilted slightly and a chub was on. But at less than 3lbs it was not the one I wanted and obviously not yet old (and wise) enough to know that suspended flake should be left alone. Get the cast right however and the technique is a deady one, bites confident and very easy to hook.

I don't always walk around a stillwater looking for signs of chub; some days I sit tight waiting for them to come to me. Here, the drill is to scatter two or three pieces of crust on the surface and wait for one to be attacked, then show the chub a piece of flake with a hook inside, with or without a float, whichever is considered best.

Providing you remain *dead* still it is surprising how close in chub will come. One day I was standing in the margins of a pit wondering what I should do when I noticed a good chub coming towards me about a yard or two out from where I was standing. I had not got a bait in the water but there was a piece of flake on the hook which I was holding in my hand. I kept still, very still, watched the chub swim past me then, when a few yards further on, I dropped the flake in the water just behind it but still under the rod top. Hearing the 'plop' the chub turned, and took it without hesitation. It weighed 4lb 1oz and was one of the easiest chub I have ever caught.

You don't *have* to use bread of course, lobworms are just as good, but whatever the bait, quietness is essential at all times; if a chub has the slightest suspicion you are there—you've had it!

Although I have said stillwater chub are difficult this does not necessarily apply to *all* stillwaters. Over the years I have fished a considerable number of stillwaters which have varied from downright difficult and soul-destroying to fairly easy. Kevin Maddocks tells me he knows several lakes where chub produce carp-like runs on floating crust, large trout pellet baits and flavoured carp baits. These, Kevin says, are easy to catch—*on carp tackle* too!

In one pit I fish the chub are fairly easy in daytime, especially when you show them floating crust; also on caster and maggot on light tackle. What I find strange about the pit however—the one mentioned at the beginning of this chapter—is that in winter, at night, you catch four-pounders, but rarely in daytime. If we catch them in winter then why not in summer?

In another pit it is not too difficult to catch a big chub but once winter sets in—that's it. Yet one day Geoff Barnes watched someone catch two biggies on float-fished maggots fished well off bottom with the strong wind blowing the float (fished double-rubber too) and bait along! Correct presentation always important?—that day it wasn't!

Catching chub on carp gear does not surprise me—in chapter 10 I tell how I nobbled a 'seven' on 20lb Dacron! It isn't the *sight* of tackle which frightens chub (or most fish for that matter) but whether it affects presentation. Nevertheless, I think it is safe to say that, generally speaking, stillwater chub are difficult. If you know a water where they are not—then count your blessings!

The author playing one of a great number of chub he caught from the Annan in Scotland.

8 The River Annan

In 1955 the capture was reported of a huge chub weighing 10½lbs from the river Annan in Scotland, the captor a Dr Cameron who had taken the great fish while salmon fishing and which was subsequently fed to a cat. Despite the fish not being produced it was accepted as a new British record, a position it held until 1968 when the list was revised and several doubtfuls, including the Doctor's chub, were erased.

Like many anglers I did not believe in the fish. Having been told it had been eaten by a cat Dick Walker went to the trouble of starving one of his cats then giving it a 3lb chub which, despite being deprived of food, was unable to finish it off. 'It must have been some cat to eat ten pounds of chub', Walker commented.

Some time later I penned an article on outsize chub and mentioned 'the reputed ten-pounder from the Annan'. To my surprise the good Doctor replied, saying that whether I believed it or not he *had* caught a ten-pound chub. So I wondered: *did* ten-pounders exist in the Annan after all; had in fact the Doctor put such a leviathan on the bank? For some time I could not get that chub, nor the Annan, out of my mind and in 1967 with my wife Sue I journeyed north to fish there.

By pure chance the first angler I met was the bailiff. Further downriver, he informed me, was a large pool unfished by salmon anglers because of the large numbers of chub present. Most reaches of the river were, he said, poisoned from time to time to remove the coarse fish; this particular pool however was never touched. Then came the sixty-dollar question; the reputed ten-pounder. To my amazement he said he had actually seen the fish which he assured me *was* a chub. But that was not all: from time to time double-figure chub had been taken when poisoning the river; not many it was true, but a few.

Now I'm always sceptical when people speak glibly about outsize fish so I asked what size of chub I could expect downstream in the pool. 'Two pounds', he replied, 'but there are plenty of five and six pounders if you can catch them'. An hour later Sue and I were at the pool.

It was a large pool some seventy yards across, but that was not all. Along the margins were countless numbers of chub; never before (nor since) had I seen so many. We approached the water carefully for the bank was low and soggy, shaking as we walked over it. Next day we were to find out why. With trembling hands I tackled up with a 6lb line, number 6 hook and a small float two inches in length carrying one swan shot. This I pushed against the float which I stopped two feet from the hook. On that I placed a large lobworm. The worm hit the water and the chub scattered. They were some time returning and five minutes later the float cocked and slid away. I struck, hooked the fish — then it was gone. Obviously they needed more time and the next time I let the float travel a little further, a gentle strike and it was on: 3½lbs.

The pool was literally swarming with chub, yet I could not get another bite and I had a feeling the float was responsible. Although the chub were not used to hooks they retained their cunning and shyness. Obviously a change of tactics was necessary. I removed both float and shot leaving just the hook and lobworm. This I cast as far as I could and retrieved in short jerks. The first cast produced a four-pounder, quickly followed by several others around three pounds. Then suddenly, the bites stopped, the chub disappeared and shortly after we packed.

Before I went, however, I crawled to the area where most of the activity had been. Two chub glided out from the shallows. I will not guess their weight but just one would have been enough to make the long journey worthwhile. Then rain began to fall.

We awoke next morning to find it still raining. Undaunted we made our way to the pool where a change had taken place. On the fast-rising river the pool was twice its size and where we had sat the previous day fish were rising. Swirls and leaps covered almost the entire area, sometimes as many as six fish showing together.

From my bank a strong wind blew towards us and a shot on the line was necessary to get the bait out. Once this touched bottom I let out a little slack and watched the line as it hung from the rod top.

There was no mistaking a bite; the line tightened rapidly, the chub almost hooking themselves.

By mid-afternoon I began to have doubts about a big one for I had by that time ten between 2½ and 3¼lbs. With fish still rising I moved to another swim fifty yards away but it was the same story and after taking five more of similar size, I packed up. The next day I took fourteen around 3lbs and went home wondering what to do the following day — our last.

On arrival I chose an area previously unfished and introduced two handfuls of groundbait some forty yards from the bank, then trotted crust and flake. I had taken four three-pounders when a very big fish rolled, so I hastily changed to a smaller float with the bait just below the surface. Still more chub but no big ones, so picking up my gear I took the long walk to the other side of the pool which I had not fished. Under the bank the plummet revealed 20ft of water with barely six feet less than twenty yards out.

I fished the deeps, the middle and surrounding areas and the fish still came but nothing above 3¾lbs. With the chub biting freely how many I might have caught had I stayed I really don't know, but I packed — for the last time.

So . . . does the Annan hold double-figure chub? Those two great fish I saw in the margins, doubles being taken during poisoning, the bailiff's accurate forecast of what I could expect in the pool — yes, I believe there is; what's more, the good Doctor did probably after all catch a ten-pounder. Whether the cat ate it all itself however is another matter!

The pool on the Annan. It was from under the branch in the foreground where the author saw two monster chub.

9 Some Big Chub Waters and Big Chub List

Chub are fairly widespread throughout the country and there are comparatively few rivers where chub of some size cannot be found. Not every river holds big chub however (by 'big' I mean 4lbs) and where very big chub (5lbs and over) are concerned, even fewer still.

Among our best chub rivers are the Hampshire Avon, Dorset Stour, Norfolk's Wissey and Wensum, the Sussex Rother, Yorkshire Ouse, Swale and Ure, Severn, Kentish Beult, Kennet, Wey, (Surrey) Thames, some parts of the Windrush, Cherwell (Oxon), the Annan and Wye.

Having not fished all these rivers I cannot say much about them but for anyone intending visiting any for the first time — or if previous visits have been unsuccessful — I say this: contact someone who knows that particular river. Among these are Ernest Leah (Dorset Stour), John Wilson (Norfolk rivers), Jim Gibbinson (Sussex and Kent rivers), Brian Moreland or Dave Plummer (Yorkshire), and — well, I might as well say it! — myself the Oxfordshire waters.

In recent years there has been considerable interest shown in outsize chub, much of which is due to the big chub now being caught in stillwaters (these I will discuss in a minute). Where outsize chub — 6lb plus — in rivers are concerned however I consider the Wye best for two reasons: (a) monster chub are undoubtedly present and (b) much of the river is confined to salmon fishing only and is never, or only rarely, coarse fished.

Having fished the river and talked to the locals I have little doubt that record busters exist in the Scottish Annan and Colin Dyson recently told me of one very big chub in the Wensum. Despite claims to the contrary I don't *think* the Thames is capable of producing a new record—which goes for all Oxfordshire rivers.

Until the dredger reared its ugly bucket the Ouse around Stony Stratford was one of our finest big-chub rivers. Dick Walker once found a freshly-dead monster weighing 8lb 2oz at Beachampton; today however, the river thanks to the dredger and abstraction is but a mere shadow of its former self. In the Ouse at Offord Dick again once found a monster chub which was too rotten to weigh but at 27ins long it must have been some fish—Dick's estimate was 10lbs. From time to time Dick has seen others in the river of similar size but whether such fish exist there today I would not like to say.

Every chub angler's dream—it's certainly mine—is to put a 'double' on the bank, so what *are* the chances of such dreams coming true—from rivers that is? Very slim I think, but if my life depended on it I would say those parts of the Wye fished exclusively for salmon and the Annan, provide the best bet.

I have already discussed Dr. Cameron's 10¼lb chub in the previous chapter and sightings of huge chub—one by Paul King in the Wye—have been reported from time to time. Dr. Cameron's fish apart, three other 'doubles' are on record, one as recent as 1981, another as far back as 1875 (see list of 'Top 50' chub).

But while our rivers continue to decline, gravel pits are on the 'up' and it will be from one of these where I believe a new record will eventually come. One of these could be Hardwick near the village of that name in Oxfordshire. This water is controlled by Gerrards Cross Angling Club but, like some privately-owned pits I have fished, is 'difficult' fishing. But outsize chub are there all right and it only needs the right man, in the right place, at the right time...

Living as I do close to a great number of gravel pits I have spent —and shall continue to spend—a lot of time fishing them. In one I have seen two chub which I would say were 'doubles'; Philip Tew and Kevin Pimm—who both know what seven-pound chub look like—tell me they too have seen similar fish, and other anglers whose words I trust have reported similar sightings.

With so much interest now being shown in gravel pits I am often asked what kind of pit one should look for. Size is not, I think, important—I have seen big chub in pits more than 60 acres and in others little more than three, but clarity is, I think. Waters where the bottom can be seen 8-10ft down and where weed growth is prolific are my

The 8lb 4oz chub taken by G. F. Smith from the Hants Avon in 1913 held the record for forty years. Many believe this should still stand as the record.

number one choice and if the water appears to hold only a small head of fish, that's better still. In short: the harder the water the more likely it is to produce an outsize chub.

In his book *Chub* (The Osprey Anglers), Jim Gibbinson says: 'Whether or not chub are capable of spawning in stillwaters I'm not sure. I suspect that the eggs and fry need running water which would appear to confine spawning to those having feeder streams. Those feeder streams are, in my opinion, responsible for the chub stocks in many stillwaters, the chub having at some time wandered from the parent river and found their way to the lake. Other stillwaters are stocked by flooding I would guess — for I know of no stillwater holding chub that isn't either fed by a feeder stream or subject to flooding. Doubtless readers know plenty and will prove me wrong!'

Jim is both right and wrong — right in saying 'no doubt readers will prove me wrong'; wrong in suggesting (although he admits he is not sure) chub do not spawn in stillwaters.

Many of the stillwaters in which I catch chub are neither fed by rivers or prone to flooding although some are adjacent to rivers. In my experience that is of little consequence. And yes, chub *do* spawn in stillwaters — only this year I came across dozens of chublets between two and four inches in the margins of one pit, and another has always had a good head of chub between one and two pounds. Both pits are cut off completely from rivers or underground streams.

The last word on the possibility of a 10lb chub being taken from a stillwater must go to Dick Walker who, in the 50's, saw two fish in Redmire. 'I only caught the small one at five pounds and some ounces', Dick said: 'its mate looked big enough to have eaten it — I'd guess at the very least twelve pounds'. Commenting on this, Jim Gibbinson said, 'Twelve pounds. Now there's a fish to dream about'. Indeed!

The list below of the 'Top 50' chub recorded contains for various reasons some 'doubtfuls'. But no matter: the list is impressive. 'You only just made the top fifty', Len Arbery said when he called at my home, which surprised me for I had no idea so many outsize chub had been recorded. As I said earlier, whether all the claims are genuine is another matter, but of one thing I am certain: Bill Warren's record fish taken from the Avon at Christchurch in 1957 is *not* the biggest chub ever landed.

The late Bill Warren with his 7lb 6oz chub, the present record.

112 FISHING FOR BIG CHUB

The 8lb 4oz fish taken by G. F. Smith of Putney from the Hampshire Avon in 1913 is one such fish. This leviathan, set up by Coopers and owned by the Red Spinners club, now resides at the home of the club's librarian Gerry Hughes.

Smith's chub held the record for nearly 40 years and is possibly the largest *authentic* chub caught in the British Isles. At the time of writing I have not seen this fish (something I must put right) but Len Arbery believes the weight could easily have been *more* than 8lb 4oz at the time of capture. Measuring 25ins overall with, I understand, an impressive girth, Len is probably right. My 6lb 6oz fish which was not particularly deep measured 23½ins; my 7lb 4oz fish I did not, unfortunately, measure but its depth in relation to its length was considerably larger than my 'six'.

TOP 50 CHUB

*13.4.0	Unknown teenager	Liddle	Mar	1972
†10.13.0	P. Morgan (Abergavenny)	Wye	Nov	1981
10.8.0	W. Cockburn	Crane		1875
§10.8.0	Dr. J. Cameron (Dumfries)	Annan	July	1955
8.12.0	J. Lewis (London)	Mole	Oct	1964
• 8.8.0	A. Smith (Birmingham)	Blyth	Aug	1980
8.8.0	D. Deeks	Sussex Rother		1951
8.4.8	A. Johnson (Christchurch)	Hants Avon	Sept	1972
8.4.0	G. F. Smith (Putney)	Hants Avon	Dec	1913
8.4.0	J. Roberts (Kings Lynn)	Wissey		1960
8.4.0	C. Smith (Wortlington)	Thames	July	1975
8.3.4	R. Thompson (Coventry)	Nene	Feb	1972
8.2.0	H. Smith (London)	Hants Avon	July	1952
» 8.1.0	M. Townsend (Oxford)	Thames	Feb	1982
8.0.0	S. Harmel (London)	Hants Avon	Aug	1964
8.0.0	Angler unknown	Olway Brook (S.Wales)		1973
8.0.0	S. Tyrer (Liverpool)	Ribble	Jan	1976
« 8.0.0	A. Sargent (Castle Bromwich)	Blythe (Staffs)	May	1976
8.0.0	D. Grady (Pershore)	Wye	June	1976
7.15.0	P. Minton (York)	Yorks Ouse	Oct	1964
7.14.8	Mrs H. Jones	Dorset Stour	Sept	1937
7.14.0	G. Worth (Birmingham)	Severn	Dec	1948

7.11.8	P. W. Hunt	Great Ouse	Dec 1938
7.10.	D. Jones (Rhymney)	S. Wales Pond	Mar 1976
7.9.8	W. Campbell (Hull)	Barmston Drain (Yorks)	1965
7.9.0	A. C. Thomas (London)	Beult	Mar 1966
7.9.0	S. Maddox (Stowmarket)	Waveney	Jan 1974
7.9.0	R. Maxey (London)	Medway	Feb 1976
7.8.0	Mr Gillett	Hants Avon	1920
7.8.0	L. Parsons	Great Ouse	Dec 1938
7.8.0	F. Hill	Hants Avon	Aug 1955
7.8.0	Maj. J. H. Peacock (Castleford)	Swale	June 1961
7.8.0	Maj. J. H. Peacock (Castleford)	Swale	June 1962
7.8.0	R. Watkins (London)	Hants Avon	Oct 1964
7.7.0	S. Harmel (London)	Hants Avon	July 1971
7.7.0	S. Pope (Barnsley)	Ure	Dec 1972
7.7.0	P. Rix (Broughton)	Wissey	May 1976
7.6.8	F. W. Smith	Hants Avon	July 1906
7.6.0	Dr. Lewis Smith	Hants Avon	Dec 1932
**7.6.0	W. Warren (Reading)	Hants Avon	1957
7.6.0	W. Hill (London)	Kennet	Feb 1963
7.6.0	R. Maxey (London)	Medway	Feb 1976
7.6.0	D. Charlton (Liverpool)	Severn	July 1977
7.5.0	E. J. Walker	Hants Avon	Aug 1904
7.5.0	J. Cairns	Kirtle (Dumfries)	Feb 1968
7.5.0	D. Heathcote (Shrewsbury)	Severn	Feb 1972
7.5.0	S. Pope (Barnsley)	Ure	Mar 1971
7.5.0	D. Laughton (Stamford)	Welland	Jan 1977
7.4.0	K. Henderson	Hants Avon	Sept 1969
7.4.0	F. W. K. Wallis (Nottingham)	Hants Avon	Aug 1913
7.4.0	J. Cadd (Oxford)	Thames	Nov 1971
7.4.0	T. Wood (Leeds)	Swale	July 1972
7.4.0	F. B. Arnold (Newbury)	Kennet	1953
7.4.0	R. Fearn (Pett's Wood)	Hants Avon	Oct 1962
7.4.0	D. Smith (Ossett)	Healey Dam (Ossett)	Sept 1966
7.4.0	K. Sismore (Stamford)	Welland	Oct 1969
7.4.0	D. Thompson (Kingston)	Thames	Aug 1979
7.4.0	K. Pimm (Eynsham)	Oxford Lake	Nov 1980
7.4.0	M. Townsend (Oxford)	Thames	Nov 1981
7.4.0	P. Stone (Oxford)	Oxford Pit	Feb 1982

114 FISHING FOR BIG CHUB

* reported in *Anglers Mail* but no photograph or name was given nor was there any later confirmation.
† believed no record claim so far made for this comparatively recent fish.
§ accepted as the record, this fish was disbelieved, rightly most seem to think, in the British Record (rod-caught) Fish Committee's 1968 re-assessment of records. Said to be taken on fly, it was never witnessed by anglers used to chub. Its acceptance as the record for 13 years however undoubtedly led to no claims from those who caught fine chub between 1955 and 1968.
• no claim made as fishery rules demanded immediate return of fish.
» no record claim was made as, according to reports at the time, the captor did not want to damage the fish. There were four witnesses.
« taken in the coarse fish close season and therefore not eligible for record claim.
** the fish currently accepted as the record by the British Record (rod caught) Fish Committee. Reckoned the doyen of chub fishers this century, the late Bill Warren had 220 chub over 5lbs, 16 over 6lbs and one, the fish in the list, over 7lbs. Although listed as living in Reading, at the time of the capture of the 7lb 6oz chub Bill Warren lived at Christchurch. Sonny Warren, Bill's brother, retains the case of this fish.

RECORD RIVER CHUB

While the above list makes clear which chub were records for the rivers they came from, the list below gives records for rivers not covered above.

Arun (Sussex)	7.0.0	S. Charman (Billingshurst)	July 1973
Avon (Bristol)	5.4.0	E. Moore (Hengrove)	July 1961
Axe (Somerset)	6.3.0	G. Martin (Weston-super-Mare)	Nov 1976
Banwy (Wales)	6.13.0	G. Smith (Sedgeley)	June 1981
Cherwell (Oxon)	7.0.0	J. Millomiss (Islip)	Oct 1962
Dee (Cheshire)	6.14.0	W. Harding (Crewe)	Nov 1974
Derwent (Yorks)	7.2.0	Angler unknown	Aug 1967
Eden (Cumbria)	6.3.0	W. Corless (Wigan)	Date unknown
Hull (Yorks)	7.0.0	A. Kemp (Hessle)	Jan 1970
Nidd (Yorks)	5.9.0	E. Stone (Knaresborough)	1963

Ribble (Lancs)	6.12.0	C. Farrell (Manchester)	Jan	1974
Roding (Essex)	6.7.0	W. Goldspink (London)	Nov	1980
Rye (Yorks)	6.12.0	F. Holgate (Bridlington)	Sept	1970
Sow (Staffs)	6.0.0	J. Davies (Stafford)	Jan	1976
Tees (Co. Durham)	5.4.0	A. Liddell (Brampton)	Feb	1977
Tone (Somerset)	6.14.0	J. Parcell (Taunton)	Aug	1975
Trent	7.2.0	F. W. K. Wallis (Nottingham)		1903
Usk (S. Wales)	5.4.0	J. Wilding (Newport)	Dec	1970
Wensum (Norfolk)	6.4.0	W. Pickard		1968
Wey (Surrey)	7.2.0	H. Truelove (Mitcham)	July	1966
Wharfe (Yorks)	6.3.0	Mr Fairley (Yorks)		1950
Windrush (Oxon)	7.1.0	J. Burrows (Burford)	Feb	1976
Wyre (Lancs)	6.10.0	A. Clarke (Blackpool)	June	1975

Geoff Barnes hooked this 5lb 7oz pit chub at the same moment that the author hooked the biggest (5lb 1oz) of the two shown on page 85.

10 My Biggest Chub

I now come to the final chapter and how I came to catch a chub which is undoubtedly the highlight of my chub fishing career.

On Friday January 18 1982 I went to the Oxfordshire pit again, arriving an hour before dark. A bitterly cold east wind was blowing but that did not matter; my determination to catch a seven pounder was stronger than ever; nothing, least of all an east wind, was going to stop me.

As I had done so many times before I tackled up with two of my 'Lite-Leger' rods, 9lb line, 20lb Dacron trace with two number 6 Pete Drennan singles attached. A few nights previously Pete had called at my home with samples of his new range of hooks. After studying a particular kind I said, 'I'll go and catch a seven-pound chub on one'. Little did I know . . .

My baits were sardines and with the memory of that chub coming in against my rod rest still clear in my mind I decided to fish the baits close in, less than five yards from the bank. Because of that I was faced with two options: either to sit close to the rods and not move, or sit against the car some ten yards away. Because of the cold wind a brolly would be necessary if I sat at the rods but I did not consider putting a brolly up wise. I would sit against the car.

It was almost dark when one bobbin lifted and dropped to the ground and I was at the rod immediately. Line was already being taken but very gently indeed; nevertheless I tightened and the rod buckled over. Unlike the pike I had caught previously the fish gave several sharp 'knocks'—chub. Two minutes later it was on the bank but a glance showed it was far removed from seven pounds and a minute later the scales showed it to be 4½lbs. For the very first time in my life I was disappointed with a four-pound chub: I had not spent all those long biteless hours fishing for a four-pounder. As I went to remove the hook I heard a disturbance. In the swim where I had just taken the chub a fish had boiled, then, as I looked, two more swirls appeared.

Disappointment was quickly forgotten, however, for as I placed it in the keepnet the other bobbin lifted. Hardly believing my eyes I put the net down and picked up the rod. It had taken me some thirty seconds to reach the rod, and line was peeling off the spool. I tightened, the rod pulled over and after remaining still for several seconds two heavy 'knocks' occurred—the same kind of 'knock' I had felt two minutes earlier. . . The fish fought strongly, twice taking several feet of line which made me wonder whether despite further 'knocks' I was after all attached to a pike. Then the fish boiled close in and I saw a pair of white lips. With shaking hands—yes, shaking—I pulled it over the net and when I lifted it ashore I knew my dream had come true.

The scales said 7lb 4oz but shaking hands are not good for establishing a correct weight so, placing it in the net, I rebaited both rods, sat back and drank a cup of coffee. For I reasoned, with two chub in the net and others obviously present there might be a chance of a third. Half an hour later, however, with no further signs of activity I decided to get the fish witnessed and photographed, and leaving my gear drove to the nearest village to phone two friends, Dennis Moss and Pete Carpenter. When they arrived I asked them to weigh the fish. 'Seven pounds five ounces', Dennis said, then weighed the plastic bag which registered an ounce. 7lb 4oz it was then.

Dennis then took some pictures but I had to be sure and decided to take more in daylight. I don't like leaving fish overnight but this was something special, and early the following morning Geoff Barnes did the honours and I slipped the fish back.

To catch a seven-pound chub by design was a great thrill for it had picked up my bait close in where it would not have been had I not seen a chub two weeks earlier against my rod rest. That, plus sightings of big chub in other pits at dawn, Kevin Pimm's account of his mackerel being picked up in 12ins of water while he was asleep, and the chub I caught against John Everard's rod rest in another pit years earlier, had shown beyond doubt that chub come in to the margins at night and that a bait fished close in stands a good chance of being taken *providing* there is no bankside disturbance.

Twenty-two years previously I had gazed in awe at the late Bill Warren's 7lb 6oz monster and wondered whether I would ever catch such a fish. At the time it was a dream, nothing more, a dream however which on that bitterly cold January night finally came true.

The author and his 7lb 4oz chub — a long-cherished ambition.

INDEX

A
Angling Times 25
Annan, River 103-105

B
Baits 10, 29-37, 43, 75-76
Behabiour 1-18
Beta-lites 25-26, 92
Big chub waters and list 107-115
bite indicators 22-24
bites 43, 45, 46, 49, 52, 65, 86, 188
bobbins 22, 97, 117

C
'Carp Fever', Kevin Maddocks 30
casters 62
cheese 30-32
cheese-paste, mixing 32
Cherwell, River 18, 50
chub chasing 99
close-in fishing 18, 98, 99, 100-101, 117
Coarse Fishing Monthly 7, 94
crayfish 76-77
crust 68-71, 89

D
Dacron 96, 97, 98, 101, 117
deadbaits 9, 11, 12, 17-18, 92-101
Drennan Feederlinks 26-27

F
feeders 54-57
flake 17, 100
flies 37
floats 17, 25-26, 73
float fishing 58, 88-92
floating crust 15, 18, 39, 68, 101
fly-fishing 33-35
free-lined flake 71-72

G
gravel pits 9, 16, 40, 83, 88, 117
groundbait 45

H
holding places 39
hooks 21, 22

I
ice-holes 79-82
instant strike rig 97

L
leads 24
legering 22, 41-57, 75, 83-88
Legerstrike rod 21
leger stops 22

lights 91-92
location 39-40
loose feeding 64, 84, 88

M
Maddocks, Kevin 30, 101
maggots 86, 89, 91, 101

P
patience 12
Pete Drennan floats 17, 24, 99
presentation 17, 101

Q
quiver-tips 50-51

R
Record Fish Committee 12
reels 21-22
Rivers 12, 41
 small 73, 77
rods 21, 54
'Royalty' 11

S
shotting 64, 65, 66-68, 72
shyness 10, 13, 16, 18
sliding links 24-25
spinning 35-36
stick float 66
stillwaters, stillwater chub 9, 10, 18, 40, 83-101, 100
'Stillwater Angling' by Dick Walker 96
strike, striking 52, 54, 70
surface feeding 14, 15

T
tackle 21-28
Thames, River 14, 15, 18, 32, 49, 59, 68, 73, 80
touch-legering 46-48, 49
trotting 58
'Twitchers' 88

U
'Ultra-lite' rod 21
upstream legering 52-53

W
'waggler' 62-66
Walker, Dick 12, 25, 40, 62, 76, 96, 103, 110
weather 10
weed 52-53, 58
weirpools 13, 37, 48-49, 72
winter 15, 49, 79-80
wire 96